# DIGITAL BLACK FEMINISM

# CRITICAL CULTURAL COMMUNICATION

General Editors: Jonathan Gray, Aswin Punathambekar, Adrienne Shaw

Founding Editors: Sarah Banet-Weiser and Kent A. Ono

# Digital Black Feminism

Catherine Knight Steele

NEW YORK UNIVERSITY PRESS

New York

NEW YORK UNIVERSITY PRESS
New York
www.nyupress.org

References to internet websites (URLs) were accurate at the time of writing. Neither the author nor New York University Press is responsible for URLs that may have expired or changed since the manuscript was prepared.

Library of Congress Cataloging-in-Publication Data

Names: Steele, Catherine Knight, author.
Title: Digital Black feminism / Catherine Knight Steele.
Description: New York : New York University Press, [2021] | Series: Critical cultural communication | Includes bibliographical references and index.
Identifiers: LCCN 2021011568 | ISBN 9781479808373 (hardback ; alk. paper) | ISBN 9781479808380 (paperback ; alk. paper) | ISBN 9781479808366 (ebook) | ISBN 9781479808397 (ebook other)
Subjects: LCSH: Internet and women—United States. | African American women. | Feminism—United States. | Technology and blacks—United States. | Technology and women—United States.
Classification: LCC HQ1178 .S74 2021 | DDC 305.48/896073—dc23
LC record available at https://lccn.loc.gov/2021011568

New York University Press books are printed on acid-free paper, and their binding materials are chosen for strength and durability. We strive to use environmentally responsible suppliers and materials to the greatest extent possible in publishing our books.

Manufactured in the United States of America

10 9 8 7 6 5 4 3 2 1

Also available as an e-book

# CONTENTS

# Introduction

## *For the Black Girls Who Don't Code*

Books about race are often about Black men, books about technology are often about white men, and books about feminism are often about white women. This book is about Black women. Studying Black women is often considered too "niche." In the early years of my career, various senior scholars advised me to study Black folks' discourse online by comparing it to whiteness. In graduate school, a faculty member suggested that my dissertation research on the Black blogosphere would be much more interesting if I compared this community of writers to recent European immigrants online. When you decide to center Black folks, Black culture, and Black discourse, this provokes questions of validity and objectivity. However, those in the dominant group who study themselves (1) never have to name their work as the study of white folks and (2) are lauded for their work's breadth and broad applicability. As was the case in graduate school—when I politely declined that faculty member's placement on my committee—I have little interest in writing a comparative analysis between Black women's use of technology and Black men's or white women's. Instead, in this book, I place Black women at the center of conceptualizing technology and digital culture. I argue that Black women's historical and persistent relationship with technology provides the most generative means of studying the possibilities and constraints of our ever-changing digital world.

Founded in 2011 by Kimberly Bryant, Black Girls CODE is a nonprofit organization that provides technology education to African American girls.[1] The group's motto is "Imagine. Build. Create." Their website continues, "Imagine a world where everyone is given the tools to succeed, and then help us build ways for everyone to access information and create a new age of women of color in technology" (https://web.archive

.org/web/20210628152208/https://www.blackgirlscode.com/what-we
-do.html). Research demonstrates that programs like Black Girls CODE
can indeed result in increased "leadership, confidence, and self-efficacy"
(Rockman, 2017, p. 18). While organizations like Black Girls CODE provide critical interventions for Black girls in STEM, I argue that Black
girls and women have long possessed the digital expertise necessary for
the future. Learning to code is neither a panacea nor the missing tool
to usurping the racism that has precluded Black women's technological
skills from being recognized by the masses. Reminding us of the profoundly troubling racism and sexism experienced by Black women in
Silicon Valley, California, Alondra Nelson asks, "Black girls code, and
then what? Do we want to send these young women into Silicon Valley
to toxic work environments?" (Nelson, 2020). Further, an overemphasis
on coding and programming skills accepts mythology about Blackness,
womanhood, and technology that does not serve Black women and girls.

The goals of *Digital Black Feminism* are twofold. The first is that we
begin to rightly position Black women online as central to the future of
communication technology. By tracing the historical relationship between Black women and technology, I reposition Black women online
as purveyors of digital skill and expertise, not deficient or in need of new
skills to survive a changing digital landscape. Black women without extensive programming experience have maximized platform affordances,
built transmedia platforms, led platform migrations, pushed platform
policy changes regarding hate speech and content moderation, and in-
troduced us to new pay structures as precursors to influencer culture.
Black feminist writer Luvvie Ajayi started her writing career with a blogging platform, *Awesomely Luvvie*. She has since developed LuvvNation,
a stand-alone social media network, and Awesomely Techie, a digital
consulting and web strategy firm. Jamilah Lemieux, an early adopter of
online media, now consults for political campaigns. Kimberly Nicole
Foster has shown bloggers how to shift content from the blogosphere to
YouTube seamlessly. Marah Lidey is one of the cofounders of Shine, a
mental health app that speaks specifically to the experiences of women
of color. As she writes, "Imagine all the ideas we're missing out on because people from more marginalized experiences—that are uniquely
positioned to solve problems because of that experience—struggle to
see themselves in existing founders" (Shine, 2020). However, this not a

problem for Black women and other marginalized communities to solve. Black women make structural alterations to digital spheres of communication through developing stand-alone apps and platforms. They are early adopters and transformers of existing platforms, and their online content already serves as models for other creatives. *Digital Black Feminism* provides the historical context needed to consider the digital turn and charts Black women's long-standing relationship to communication technology as a mechanism to better understand the future of our digital world.

The second goal of *Digital Black Feminism* is to document a shift in Black feminist principles and praxes and ensure we consider digital Black feminist thinkers' online writing as central to the ongoing work of liberation. As Feminista Jones writes, "Who could have predicted that people who never set foot on a college campus, much less in a specialized journalism school, would have international audiences reading their cultural and sociopolitical analyses? Or have their work be part of a rigorous academic curriculum at universities they could never afford to attend?" (Jones, 2019a, p. 6). Black feminist thinkers have always existed outside of the academy. However, this generation's use of digital tools and social media platforms has led some to disregard their work as part of a neoliberal superstructure, devaluing what they create online. As Brittney Cooper explains, "There is still a dearth of real knowledge about Black women public intellectuals" (B. C. Cooper, 2017, p. 145). Lifestyle blogging, natural hair tutorials, online snark, and perfectly placed memes do not mark digital Black feminists as superficial or untethered to serious scholarship. None of these practices exclude them from liberation work. They locate their spaces of retreat alongside their activist work, often earning their living by using tools of a digital capitalistic superstructure. As Cooper concludes, "Black women are serious thinkers, and it is our scholarly duty to take them seriously" (B. C. Cooper, 2017, p. 152). Black girls who may not code still possess a knowledge of and ability to navigate digital platforms. Their relationship with digital tools and culture is changing how we view technology today. In the chapters that follow, I analyze the content of digital Black feminist thought online and the mechanisms of production and dissemination, dealing with the messy complexities of a new form of Black feminism imbued with the ethos of digital praxis.

## Are #BlackGirlsMagic?

Now, perhaps more than ever, it is imperative that we attune our gaze to digital Black feminism. As the public is becoming more aware of algorithmic bias, influencer culture, the gig economy, fake news online, and social media harassment, researchers continue to point to a disproportionate impact on Black women. Safiya Noble (2018) began her inquiry into algorithmic bias with a simple question: What happens when you google search "Black girls"? In *Algorithms of Oppression*, she details how the creation and utilization of algorithms in nearly every aspect of our digital lives perpetuate anti-Black racism and misogynoir.[2] Writing for *Forbes*, Janet Burns (2017) penned, "Black Women Are Besieged on Social Media, and White Apathy Damns Us All." In her article, she describes and documents the extensive and pervasive nature of online harassment of Black women on Twitter and other social media platforms following the very public online harassment of comedienne Leslie Jones. In 2019, the *BBC*, *Washington Post*, *GQ*, and other news outlets reported that Russian internet trolls targeted African Americans to reduce voter turnout in the 2016 presidential election. Even as Black women influencers pushed platforms and challenged norms in the industry, *Adweek* admitted in 2020, "We're Sorry for Not Listening to Black Influencers before: We Expect to Be Called Out" (Pomponi, 2020). As the headlines bear out, Black women are already at the center of digital studies whether our research has followed suit.

Black women operate online and in digital spaces in ways that far surpass the possibilities imagined for them. Simultaneously, they are met online with many of the most insidious forms of sexism and racism. Black feminism is the means to unseat the oppressive forces in society that harm everyone, not only Black women. As the Combahee River Collective explained, "If Black women were free, it would mean that everyone else would have to be free since our freedom would necessitate the destruction of all the systems of oppression" (Combahee River Collective, 1983, p. 7). As bell hooks (2000a) states directly, Black feminism is for everyone. In *Digital Black Feminism*, I explore the principles, praxes, and products of digital Black feminism. In the chapters that follow, I provide an analysis of both the content and the form of Black feminist work. The use of online technology by Black feminist thinkers has changed the outcome and possibilities of Black feminist thought in the digital age, and Black feminist thought has simultaneously changed the technologies themselves. Black women's technological capability and their utility of online platforms crafting intentional discourses of resistance are predicated upon a historically unique position of having to exist in multiple worlds, manipulate various technologies, and maximize their resources. Indeed, I am making the case that we should listen to Black women.

The phrases *listen to Black women* and *ask Black women* became popularized after the election of the forty-fifth president.[3] Exposed to the same rhetoric and often living in similar economic conditions, Black women made a different choice for president than their white counterparts. Black women voted for Donald Trump in lower numbers than any other racial/gender population (Pew Research Center, 2018). The phrase *listen to Black women* has been adopted by activists, allies, and journalists who point to Black women's voting record in presidential and local elections. Twitter users created memes to remind the public that *Black women keep trying to save America from itself.* However, popularized phrases and hashtags lauding Black women for their decisions do not do the work of explaining the centuries of wisdom, labor, and ingenuity that have put Black women in a position to do the long-suffering and thankless task of attempting to save America from itself. As Treva Lindsey writes, "Black women and femmes keep developing radical ideas about social transformation, wrestling with the ways anti-Blackness manifests in areas such as the criminal justice system, health care, news media and popular culture, and tirelessly amplifying the experiences of Black women, girls and femmes. But even as our ideas are coopted, our victimization remains on the margins" (Lindsey, 2020, para. 3). As is the case with many hashtaggable lines, phrases like *listen to Black women* often do little more than virtue signal without a requirement of follow-through in terms of Black feminist praxes or principles.

Black women consistently do the *radical* work of calling for the U.S. to make right its promise of democracy. As political strategist Zerlina Maxwell explains in her book *The End of White Politics*, it is time for the left to understand that the future of politics is women of color. Nevertheless, in the months and years that followed the 2016 election, liberal and progressive politicians and writers produced think pieces lamenting the party's inability to reach white working-class men. Rather than figuring out how to maintain, grow, and energize the core and most reliable part of the democratic base, they ignored Black women. In 2016, Black women were exposed to trolls, bots, and fake news stories on social media. Indeed, they were often the target of such campaigns of disinformation. So what if liberal politicians and progressive writers asked Black women how we made political calculations amid a barrage of fake news and disinformation? What if we inquired about Black women's relationship with social media and technology, a relationship that did not shield us from exposure but provided a skill set to navigate trolling and hate speech online? What if we tried to learn how the history of Black women's use of technology and long-developed skills in intra- and intercultural communication better equipped us to be purveyors of social media, making better decisions for ourselves and society? Are Black women *really* just magic?

The phrase *Black Girl Magic* was popularized by CaShawn Thompson in 2013 when she first tweeted the hashtag #BlackGirlsAreMagic to celebrate the everyday ways that Black women thrive despite the boundaries erected to keep us from doing such. While users tweet the phrase to celebrate Oscar wins and Super Bowl halftime concerts, Black Girl Magic is indicative of the ordinary everyday "magic" of existing as a Black woman. As Thompson explained, "As a kid, I was really introverted, and I loved fairytales. I had a big imagination and all these magical ideas that weren't rooted in reality, and when I saw the women in my family running businesses, raising families, making a way out of no way, to me as a little girl, it just seemed like magic. As a child, I literally thought that Black women were magic" (Flake, 2017). Black women were doing things that white Western culture was deeply committed to teaching us that we were incapable of doing—mothering, being students, cooking healthy meals, working out, organizing for justice, being beautiful. The phrase created visibility for writers, artists, and businesswomen, but it was also reserved for semiprivate moments of celebration online. Students would post pictures of themselves on graduation day and hashtag Black Girl Magic. Sister-friends would snap a moment over brunch, adding to the Instagram pages with the captions #BlackGirlMagic.

So Black Girl Magic is not descriptive of an inexplicable supernatural power possessed by Black women. As Feminista Jones writes, "We do not have to be supernatural or superhuman to be magic—we just need to *be*" (Jones, 2019c; italics added). Black Girl Magic is the shorthand for the centuries of experience Black women have in doing everything for everyone while maintaining dignity and not sweating out their edges. This book seeks to unpack the magic of Black women who, particularly in their use of online technology, create possibilities for themselves. By examining the discourse of Black feminism as it is understood and discussed online, I demonstrate that the principles, praxes, and products of digital Black feminism are revolutionary. In so doing, I also make connections between this new form of Black feminism and the driving force behind its proliferation, the ability to be profitable. Digital technology has brought Black feminist thought to the masses, creating opportunities for freedom building while simultaneously erecting significant boundaries.

## Black Women Are Online

For years in internet studies and new media research, persons of color, and specifically Black American users, were only discussed based on a perceived lack of access to digital resources. Digital divide research predominated scholarly inquiry into the habits and uses of technology by Black persons in the U.S. By the late 2000s, some researchers argued that Black users were operating in largely unknown spaces online, and quantitative analysis of user trends missed their activity (Brock, 2009; Everett, 2009). In the early 2010s, Pew research confirmed that Black and African American use of social media was higher than whites (A. Smith, 2010). Black users often engaged with social media using smartphones, which partly explained why digital divide research focused on broadband and computer access missed their presence. In the years that followed, scholars of Black rhetoric, discourse, and internet studies have pushed for research to explore the construction of Black social movements (Freelon et al., 2018), patterns of oral culture in its migration to online space (Florini, 2013), and Black publics and counterpublics online (Steele, 2018). In the last several years, the work of Safiya Noble (2018), Charlton McIlwain (2019), Ruha Benjamin (2019), Sarah Florini (2019), and André Brock (2020) has effectively created a new genre of books that focus directly on race, Blackness, and technology. However, even with this nuanced and impactful work, internet research still often assumes a homogeneous Black online population or uses Black men as a proxy for Blackness writ large.

Kishonna Gray (2015), Sarah Jackson et al. (2020), Sherri Williams (2015), and Moya Bailey (2021), among others, have produced significant research regarding Black women's use of digital technology and Black cyberfeminism. Safiya Noble and Brendesha Tynes's (2016) *Intersectional Internet* provides an edited volume of work on the topic. Tracy Curtis's (2015) *New Media in Black Women's Autobiography* considers autobiographical narratives of Black women as means to examine the importance of the Black female body, drawing comparisons between the literary text and the use of selfies and Instagram. Writing for the public, Feminista Jones (2019a) uses her years of experience organizing online to trace critical trajectories in Black digital culture in the book *Reclaiming our Space*. Likewise, Mikki Kendall's (2020) *Hood Feminism* traces the development of Black feminist praxis for a lay audience. Even as these scholars and writers push for more focus on Black women, there is a challenge in capturing the complexity of digital Black feminists' relationship to technology.

Digital Black feminists are a diverse group of women, men, and nonbinary folks. There is no monthly meeting or club within which parties agree about tactics, strategies, and goals. They support different candidates in primaries, endorse differing policy recommendations for ending police brutality, and have sharply differing views on whether Issa and Lawrence should get back together.[4] Instead of pretending this book is a complete rendering of all Black feminist activity online, I position *Digital Black Feminism* as a report of the cultural shift happening in Black feminist discourse and society's relationship with technology. Further, as the following chapters bare out, Black feminist thought work has forever altered digital communication technologies.

## From Hip-Hop Feminism to Digital Black Feminism

As I was beginning to write this book, an encounter with a senior Black feminist scholar reminded me of the importance of naming and documenting generational and cultural shifts in Black feminist thought and praxis. During the U.S. Senate confirmation hearings for Justice Brett

Kavanaugh in 2018, I told her that I was not following the hearings online that day. Like many folks in my generation, I am always plugged in, checking updates on multiple apps and watching livestreams as I walk between buildings on campus. I explained that as a politics and news junkie, it was challenging to unplug from my phone and updates on Twitter. Still, for many reasons, some so personal I did not share, I was proud of the decision. I provided myself care instead of shouldering through the unnecessary pain of hearing the public dismissal of credible claims of sexual assault against a man who was almost certain to gain a lifetime appointment to the highest court in the land. As I discuss in chapter 3, digital Black feminist principles prioritize self-care for Black women who frequently encounter violence online. Inundated with harmful images, harassment, and violent rhetoric on social media, many digital Black feminists have determined that breaks from the news are a necessary practice of self-care. While I was steadfast in my newly found strength to protect my mental health, my colleague shamed my "lack of political engagement" and "inability to understand the significance of the moment" because of my age. She deemed this moment of self-care and extension of Black feminist praxis as childish and selfish. This little anecdote reminds me of how profound the gap can be between some Black feminist foremothers and newer iterations of Black feminism. Though we may have the same or similar goals, digital technology and Black feminism's convergence yields different principles and praxes. Digital Black feminists must contend with pushback to their differing practices from those hostile to Black feminism and those with whom they share goals. I consider this disconnect replicative of what many hip-hop feminists encountered as they argued for a more nuanced and complex Black feminism for the hip-hop generation in the 1990s.

A term coined by Joan Morgan (2000), hip-hop feminism has been theorized primarily outside of the academy.[5] Scholars like Brittney Cooper, Treva Lindsey, and Aisha Durham are also ensuring this critical development in Black feminist discourse is not overlooked in scholarly research. Durham defines *hip-hop feminism* as "a socio-cultural, intellectual, and political movement grounded in the situated knowledge of women of color from the post-civil rights generation who recognize culture as a pivotal site for political intervention to challenge, resist and mobilize collectives to dismantle systems of exploitation" (Durham, 2007,

p. 306). Lindsey describes hip-hop feminist theory as a "generationally specific and historically contingent iteration of intersectionality and of critical race feminist theory" (Lindsey, 2014, p. 54), pointing to Gloria Anzaldúa, Patricia Hill Collins, Kimberlé Crenshaw, and bell hooks as the foremothers who made hip-hop feminism possible. Like hip-hop feminism, digital Black feminism is also a generationally specific and historically contingent iteration of Black feminist thought. The development of this new Black feminist ethos and discursive practice happens in conjunction with the transformation of digital technology. Morgan explains that hip-hop feminism lies in the uncomfortable "shades of gray" that require Black feminists to reconcile their principles and praxes. Explaining the intercession of hip-hop feminism, Morgan says, "We need a feminism that possesses the same fundamental understanding held by any true student of hip-hop. The keys that unlock the riches of contemporary black female identity lie . . . at the magical intersection where those contrary voices meet—the juncture where 'truth' is no longer black and white but subtle, intriguing shades of gray" (D. A. Jackson, 2018). Morgan's "shades of gray" construct is one of the primary interventions of hip-hop feminism. Digital Black feminists also wrestle with shades of gray. Like hip-hop feminists before them, digital Black feminists work to reconcile economic and sexual freedom for themselves with community interests that may conflict with their individual needs. However, instead of *hip-hop* as a driving force, the "gray" for digital Black feminist praxis is deconstructing white supremacist capitalist patriarchy within digital culture.

## Writing about "Us"

This text focuses on Black feminism and Black women in a U.S. context. Globally, marginalized communities share many experiences with oppression and colonization and use communication technologies as resistance. However, the social history of Black womanhood is unique in American society. Black American women have a technological capability built on the legacy of enslavement, rebellion, and resilience in the U.S. context. It was from this legacy that Black American women learned the skills to craft intentional discourses of resistance online. Carole Boyce Davies (2002) rightly advises that centering the history of

American Black women's writing falls short of understanding the diasporic nature of Blackness. While I hope that this work has extensions beyond the U.S., I do not aim to capture that broad diasporic tradition of Black women writers and thinkers across the globe in this text. Nor could I explore all the differentiated relationships with technology Black women have based on geographically and culturally specific histories. Instead, I focus on the unique history of Black women living in the U.S. from the antebellum period to the present, arguing that this legacy is worthy of sustained attention over multiple books and across multiple authors. My own ancestry also influences my intentional focus on the legacy of enslavement and resistance in the U.S. context. I can trace my mother's lineage back to Germany and Denmark to the 1600s, while my father's side stops abruptly on a plantation in Virginia in 1860 with Lucinda "Granny Cindy" Jennings. My dad was born less than a hundred years later. His great-grandmother was enslaved in this country, and her great-great-granddaughter is privileged to write about the journey.

I borrow my approach to writing about Black women in part from Patricia Hill Collins and Joan Morgan. Collins, in her pivotal volume *Black Feminist Thought* (2009), makes the case that using the pronouns "we," "us," and "our" rather than "they" and "them" when referencing Black women is a political decision. Collins dismisses false flags of objectivity or rigor. Instead, she argues that separating herself from the Black women she writes about suggests an ambivalence about a subject matter to which she is deeply personally connected. I share this view. I am a Black woman and Black feminist thinker who is writing about digital Black feminism. My work is grounded in rigorous social scientific and humanistic research and my deep and abiding love of Black folks. My decision not to separate myself from those I write about acknowledges the shared knowledge construction at the core of Black feminist epistemology. As Morgan demonstrated in *When Chickenheads Come Home to Roost* (2000), the academy benefits from remaining connected to the women who do the work of refashioning Black feminism every day through their lived experiences. The Black feminist thinkers I write about create knowledge alongside me. I remain grateful for the opportunity to be counted as a part of this community.

I resist the impulse to name individual writers or thinkers as digital Black feminists. Many individuals whose writing I track in this book have never labeled themselves as such. Some do not call themselves Black feminists, instead preferring the label of womanist or no label at all. It is not my intention in this text to therefore ascribe this label to their person. Instead, I am interested in communication patterns, practices, and experiences that shape decisions about online writing, social activism, blogging, signifying, and advocating for Black feminist ideals and freedoms in digital work and play. The women, men, and nonbinary folks who do this work are, I argue, *doing* digital Black feminism. This text provides a moment to understand the patterns in their discourse, their challenges to the status quo, and the obstacles they face as made explicit in the tweets, posts, videos, and memes they leave behind. Many of our grandmothers would never have considered themselves Black feminists, yet this does not deny their labor and words as a foundational part of Black feminist praxis. Likewise, I draw our attention to the digital artifacts to which we have so generously been granted access. Rather than determining who can lay claim to this new moniker, I am interested in what digital Black feminism might *do*.

This book focuses exclusively on the discourse created online and offline and how technology mitigates that discourse. I study what Black feminist thinkers leave behind rather than directly asking them about their relationships with technology. While interviews are an essential tool in a researcher's tool kit, it is difficult to interrogate ourselves about how our use of digital technology influences what we say and do in online spaces. This book traces the digital turn in Black feminist thought and therefore requires a critical analysis of discourse alongside a parallel study of technology's form and function.[6] I apply the same approach to both digital Black feminists and Black feminist thinkers of the twentieth century, using their artifacts (tweets, diary entries, Instagram posts, and letters) as means to trace the long historical relationship with technology. I spent six years intentionally collecting blog posts, tweets, Instagram Stories, and Facebook posts for this book, following hundreds of Black feminist public scholars on multiple platforms, and many more years participating as a member of their discursive communities. While I have built relationships with some, I know many more by collecting their online work. I do not extract tweets or posts without context, "scrape" platforms, or analyze massive data sets because doing so would undermine my ability to conduct deep readings of these texts. Instead, I position myself both as a researcher in the field and as a group member, yielding access to both the digital artifacts and the context required to interpret them.

Reading work as it is published and engaging with quickly vanishing Instagram Stories as I would a conversation observed in the field require a long-term commitment to a group that does not end when this book is published. Writing about communities that experience marginalization and oppression requires long-term commitment. Though I am part of the group I study, I am not immune from considering the ethics of writing about Black women. As an academic researcher, my position can distance me from those I cite in the book. In specific spaces and with a specific audience, my position and credentials imbue my work with the credibility that the digital Black feminist writers I cite in this book must fight to attain. Therefore, it is imperative that I do not cause further harm or violence to Black women from this position of relative privilege and instead situate their public writing and scholarship alongside my own. Using the tools we study and being a part of the communities we investigate are not hindrances or biases to overcome. Recognizing my position and operating transparently in that space, I use my relationship to Black feminism and Black feminist praxis and my participation in Black feminist online discursive communities as support rather than obstacles in defining digital Black feminism.

## Why Digital Black Feminism?

In considering both the title of this book and a way to describe the kind of feminist work I am most interested in, I had to wade through a variety of naming conventions. In the past, I have used the terms *womanism* and *Black feminism* interchangeably, seeing them as merely a semantic difference with little consequence. In doing so, I had also adopted the idea that womanism and Black feminism were responsive to notable absences in mainstream white feminism. However, this position conflates the terms and ignores the political value of reclaiming the term *feminism* for Black women. As I will unpack further in the chapter that follows, Black feminism is not a subcategory of mainstream (white) feminism. Instead, Black feminism is a political choice that bolsters the claim that feminism practiced without adherence to racial politics is not feminism at all.

In the 1970s, Alice Walker used the term *womanism* to describe how Black women saw themselves in contrast to white women's activism. The origin of the word comes from a reference to the behavior of young girls as "womanish." Collins explains, "Womanish girls acted in outrageous, courageous, and willful ways, attributes that freed them from the conventions long limiting white women" (Collins, 2009, p. 10). Walker (2004) famously wrote, "Womanist is to feminist as purple is to lavender" (p. xii), positioning womanism as a more universalizing element under which feminism might fall. Monica Coleman explains, though, that over time, womanism diverged from Alice Walker's original definition to one that seems more restricted based on cisgenderedness and sexuality. As she explains, "To put it in anecdotal terms, when I tell my Black male friends that I'm a womanist, they think of me as a Black churchwoman, which I sometimes am. When I tell them that I am a Black feminist, they get a little uneasy, because they start to wonder if I'm aligned with lesbians, if I'm going to question their power, and if I'm going to call God 'She'—all of which I also do. I find the word *feminist*, whether modified by *Black* or not, to have the disruptive effect that I want" (Coleman et al., 2006, p. 92). For Coleman, Black feminism is powerful because it disrupts political forces of oppression, including heteronormativity, transphobia, homophobia, and biphobia. The intentional disruption and discomfort the term *feminism* provokes are precisely what makes *digital Black feminism* a useful term. Digital Black feminism is disruptive to mainstream white feminism and the Black feminism of the 1970s and 1980s.

I use the term *digital* instead of *cyber* to likewise disrupt cyber studies that place Black women on the periphery. Cyberfeminism or technofeminism may address women in internet technologies, but they fail to capture race and other identifiers that must also be at the forefront of analysis. Daniels, commenting on the work of cyberfeminist scholars of the 1990s, explains, "Some cyberfeminists contend that the Internet shifts gender and racial regimes of power through the human/machine hybridity of cyborgs (Haraway, 1985), identity tourism (Nakamura, 2002; Turkle, 1997), and the escape from embodiment (Hansen, 2006; Nouraie-Simone, 2005 . . .), I argue that the lived experience and actual Internet practices of girls and self-identified women reveals ways that they use the Internet to transform their material, corporeal lives in a number of complex ways that both resist and reinforce hierarchies of gender and race" (Daniels, 2009, p. 101). Daniels repositions the work of cyberfeminism from an interrogation of a postmodern experience of the feminine body to an examination of structural changes to hierarchies of gender and race. It is a useful shift that focuses on both subordination and agency in digital technology creation and use. Gray argues that Black cyberfeminism "may address the critique that traditional virtual feminist frameworks do not effectively grasp the reality of all women and may help theorize the digital and intersecting lives of women" (Gray, 2015, p. 176). Gray's "Black cyberfeminism" blends Black feminist thought and cyberfeminist theory, creating a better tool to understand Black women's use of the internet. Both Daniels and Gray recognize the shortcomings of cyberfeminism and the need to create a more inclusive space to consider the lived experiences of nondominant groups. However, even in this vital intercession, Black cyberfeminism remains bound to the lineage of cyberfeminism that excludes Black women's voices. Instead, I argue for an analytical tool that *centers* Black women in digital studies rather than advocating for our inclusion.

This brings us to digital Black feminism, which I position neither as a corrective measure to other forms of feminist inquiry nor as an extension of previous waves of feminist activism or research.[7] Digital Black feminism does not suggest that we should examine Black women's lives *too*. Instead, digital Black feminism insists we centralize Black women in our definition of and history of digital technology. Digital Black feminism is a mechanism to understand how Black feminist thought is altered by and alters technology. Digital Black feminism suggests we attune our gaze to Black women because they potentially provide the most robust site of inquiry as digital scholars interested in digital communication's capacities and constraints. "Instead of smoothing out the bugs," as Alexis Lothian and Amanda Phillips write about in their own revolutionary academic practice #TransformDH, I am interested in how digital Black feminism may "rattle the poles of the big tent" of internet inquiry "rather than slip seamlessly into it" (Lothian & Phillips, 2013). Digital Black feminism does not operate from the assumption that whiteness is the standard within technology and that Blackness or Black womanness is the deviant other. Instead, I suggest that a conception of the digital that reconsiders history and futures through the lens of Black feminist thought is vital to the future of digital communication. As Marisa Parham suggests, "What kind of critical structures might be distilled from thinking about technological adoption as itself a kind of Black cultural practice?" (Parham, 2019, para. 1). "Listen to Black women" must be more than a catchphrase. Black women are not responsible for saving anyone, but our relationship with technology, both digital and analog, provides a road map by which those interested and accountable might save themselves.

This book is organized into five chapters. In the first chapter, I begin long before the advent of digital technology to consider how Black women's specific institutional and social oppression has resulted in continued strength with communication technology. Black womanhood's social history in American society is unique. In a white supremacist and patriarchal arrangement, Black women are effectively at the bottom of the state and economic power structure while simultaneously serving as the foundation upon which the U.S. builds its empire. Therefore, the labor, creativity, and ingenuity of Black women are foundational to the fabric of the U.S. In this chapter, I rely on historical texts, including narratives, historical reconstructions, and existing literature about Black women's technology use in the antebellum period through the twentieth century. I argue that Black women's labor and lives in this period were distinct from white women's based on their mastery of labor technologies and oral culture and distinct from Black men's based on their mastery of feminized practices of communication. This historical background provides the impetus for the central argument of this text. Black women's relationship with communication technology informs a circumstance of its use that inherently is the most generative. Listening to Black women requires engagement with these complicated histories and complex arguments.

Following this history, I introduce the virtual beauty shop in chapter two. The virtual beauty shop provides a mechanism for us to interrogate a Black feminist technoculture wherein we no longer treat Black women's use and manipulation of digital technologies as deviant, deficient, or an aberration. I use the beauty shop metaphor to demonstrate the importance of a separately constructed space intentionally created for and by Black women. The shop is an independently viable institution within the Black community and one of the few spaces where Black women could own and operate a business enterprise that was not dependent on whites' patronage. I use this chapter to develop the text's theoretical and analytic framework, applying a critical cultural approach based principally on the interrelationship of three theories / significant departures in the literature. They are Patricia Hill Collins's matrix of domination, Joan Morgan's hip-hop feminism, and Anna Everett's Black technophilia. Positioning Black feminism as merely responsive to white womanhood and white feminism assumes whiteness is both the default and the origin of womanhood and feminism. If technoculture reifies whiteness, this provides no space to consider Black women's artful manipulation of communicative technology for their own purposes. Instead, the virtual beauty shop offers us a way to understand how Black feminists have created a relationship with agency, community, and profit in a digital context that mirrors their offline practices.

Following these two chapters, I trace the principles, praxes, and products of digital Black feminism. In chapter three, I propose five *principles* that make up a new era of Black feminist thought and discourse online. Using an analysis of Black feminist bloggers, I argue that digital Black feminist principles shape and are shaped by the interface and affordances of the platform where they emerge, the blogosphere. Unlike the often harassing and toxic culture of Twitter today, Black feminist blogging in the 2000s and 2010s provided a space for Black feminist thinkers to make modifications to Black feminist rhetoric within the safety of enclaved communities of discourse. Within these discursive communities, bloggers developed principles that we now see on multiple digital platforms and in the public speeches and writing of Black feminists today. The principles are the prioritization of agency, the reclamation of the right to self-identify, the centralization of gender nonbinary spaces of discourse, the creation of complicated allegiances, and the insertion of a dialectic of self and community interests. For each, I describe their deployment online and their utility in creating Black feminist discursive practices online that differentiate digital Black feminist discourse from other forms of feminism. The principles are developed through the play and everyday discourse of Black lifestyle, relationship, and hair blogs. Digital Black feminists in the blogosphere intentionally conflate the professional and personal and wrestle publicly with a complicated relationship to capitalism. Any discussion of Black digital culture and social media would be remiss not to begin by thinking about the importance of the blogosphere in making Black technoculture possible.

Next, I consider praxis. Using the archival materials of Black feminist thinkers from the twentieth century (Ida B. Wells-Barnett, Zora Neale Hurston, and Anna Julia Cooper) and a curated digital collection of publicly accessible documents (tweets, and Instagram Stories, and Facebook posts) from three digital Black feminist thinkers of the twenty-first century (Luvvie Ajayi, Jamilah Lemieux, and Feminista Jones), I place historical figures in Black feminist thought in conversation with digital Black feminist writers of today. Tracing their reflections on their public work and knowledge production, I discuss the cultural practices and ingenuity that transform their discourse based on the reformation of technology to meet their needs. The creation and dissemination of Black feminist thought online (specifically in social media and the blogosphere) is a complication and conflation of written work and oral culture. Capturing, publishing, and threading/stitching are three forms of Black feminist praxis that have existed for centuries. However, digital tools mark a shift from previous mechanisms used to conceptualize Black feminist rhetoric. This chapter charts the shift that has changed Black feminist writing in meaningful ways.

Finally, after first analyzing digital Black feminist principles and Black feminist thinkers' relationship to technology in analog and digital spaces, I examine Black feminism online as a *product*, considering branding, content creation, and audience. Returning to the metaphor of the beauty shop, I explore digital Black feminism as a business model and the implications of a consumer-based digital culture on the work of Black feminists online. The original influencers and branding experts, using Twitter, Instagram, and paid platforms like Patreon, digital Black feminists demonstrate their skill in designing brands for themselves online. They navigate the digital artifacts like viral videos and hashtags as incomplete stand-ins for rich critical analysis. They also engage in practices like prototyping to refine Black feminism online. In the transition to a consumerist digital culture, I explore what may be lost when Black feminism is a product manufactured for others' consumption and why a renewed vigilance is required to protect Black feminist thought. Rather than critique any individual's relationship with capitalism, I conclude with a path forward for a digital Black feminist future for researchers and the public.

Before a sustained engagement with the digital, I begin by charting Black women's unique history in the U.S., which created a skill set unlike their white female or Black male peers—equipping them with the ability to survive and maximize resources. If we are to listen to Black women, we must begin long before they began blogging or tweeting. We must engage in the complicated and challenging legacy of white supremacy and patriarchy, which shaped Black women living in the Americas.

1

# A History of Black Women and Technology, or Badges of Oppression and Positions of Strength

American English is a language reliant on contrasts, binaries, and opposites. In teaching language to children, our investment in these binaries becomes even more apparent. We teach children to understand descriptors by placing them in opposition to one another: up to down, in to out, girl to boy, and Black to white. As Patricia Hill Collins explains, binaries create the ideas of not only difference but opposition. "Whites and Blacks, males and females, thought and feelings are not contemporary counterparts—they are fundamentally different entities related only through their definitions as opposites" (Collins, 2009, p. 77). Gender and racial binaries have provided a basis in the U.S. for laws, norms, expectations, opportunities, and even identity construction. Gender norms in the early Americas imposed codes of conduct for white women, which white men used to justify the women's lessened resources, privileges, laws, and possibilities. The fluidity of gender that existed (and still exists) in Indigenous societies, parts of western Africa, Indonesia, India, and ancient Greece (Zimman et al., 2014) was shunned in the construction of Americanized constructs of masculinity and femininity. Instead, doctors and parents in the U.S. assign gender at birth based on a perceived biological difference. Society, therefore, became invested in the idea that white women and white men are fundamentally different based on gender. Therefore, law, property, and labor functioned differently for men and women in a U.S. context.

Likewise, racial binaries place Blackness as the perpetual foe and opponent to whiteness. In a U.S. context, our need for bicameral differentiation results from the shift from indentured servitude to chattel slavery. Within our binary system of race, the U.S. has historically assigned newcomers a place in one of the two racial groups that formed the basis of our economic and political system. New immigrants to the

U.S. find themselves in the predicament of fitting into this binary, at times working to secure their position by distancing themselves from *deviant* Blackness. Chinese immigrants, Italian immigrants, and Indian immigrants have at various points worked through the challenge of this two-part racial order, making their collective case that Blackness was, in fact, not an appropriate classifier (Loewen, 1988; Roediger, 2006; Waters, 1990). Even as race categories on the U.S. census have shifted over time to match current social and economic conditions, many immigrants still fight to be categorized as anything but Black. They distance themselves—perhaps without malicious intent but to the same effect—from the legacy of chattel slavery, hoping (potentially) to avoid the discrimination and bias attached to Black skin. Black folks in the U.S. survive and form a cultural community within a circumstance where others see Black skin, Black phenotypic markers, and perhaps most significantly, Black history as things to be overcome, transcended, or shunned. Black women contend with both gender and racial binaries that place them in subordinate positions.

To understand how Black feminists use technology, we must first interrogate how Black womanness comes to be and why Black feminist thought work continues to function as a survival strategy. In this chapter, I consider how white women and Black men have secured their positions in the racial and gender hierarchy by positioning themselves in opposition to Black womanhood. It is unusual in a book about digital technology to spend the first chapter in this way. However, before considering Black feminist blogging, social media use, or online discourse, we must reimagine our definition of technology to reinsert Black women into a history from which we have been removed. Taken from Suzanne Lebsock's (1985) book *The Free Women of Petersburg*, this chapter's title points to the duality of Black women's unique role in the American experiment. Our very oppression has served as the mechanism by which we generate ingenuity, technological capability, and strength. While digital Black feminism is for everyone, it is the lived experience, writing, and thought work of Black women that make Black feminism accessible to multiple races and genders. As such, digital Black feminism begins by considering Black feminist thought as a product of this historically binary system of race and gender wherein Black women are marginalized but still function as an integral part of the American technological machine. After linking the history of race and gendered oppression to the history of technological development, I position Black women as technological innovators, laborers, and creative manipulators of feminized communication, differentiating them from their white female counterparts and their Black male peers.

## Reconstructing Black Women's Narratives about Technology

To understand Black women's unique experience with technology, I draw from historians who consider race and gender in the early Americas. Scholars debate whether distinctly American systems like chattel slavery and U.S. capitalism are responsible for sexism and racism in the States or if these systems predate the formation of the U.S. and are a legacy of our precolonial past. While these disciplinary discussions may be of interest to some, more valuable to this discussion of Black feminist thought are the assumptions these debates make visible. Too often, historians have used the gender-neutral term Blacks (or "slaves") to mean men exclusively, and too often, we examine the construction of femininity, gender, and patriarchy by centralizing the lives of white women (Brown, 1998). Moving Black women from the margins to the center changes the parameters of the conversation altogether.

Some of Black women's erasure from American history is due to the scarcity of resources historians have to understand Black women's subjective experience.[1] Patricia Hill Collins reminds us, though, "the shadow obscuring [a] complex Black women's intellectual tradition is neither accidental nor benign" (Collins, 2009, p. 5). Too often considered a "problem" (Williams, 1987), Black women are geniuses thrown away (Walker, 1983). Technology is central to the American experiment. Yet technological expertise has been defined and documented in intentionally exclusionary ways. Those in power defined technology and wrote its history, prioritizing the written word and excluding so much of the oral history of Black women who lived through an era of state-sanctioned terrorism and enslavement. For much of our short three-hundred-year history, the master narrative of American efficiency, progress, and democracy intentionally removed marginalized groups' lives and experiences. Without a written record kept and maintained by Black women, we must examine their use of technology between the lines of the historical record.

To centralize Black women and Black feminism in a discussion of technology, I take lessons from critical archival studies (Caswell, 2016). Tonia Sutherland defines archival amnesty as "American archivists' neglect in documenting violence against a marginalized group [that] has real and lasting implications for restorative and transitional justice" (Sutherland, 2017, p. 7). Archival amnesty is a mechanism we can use to critique bias and absences in the contemporary historical record that do not serve a master narrative (Sutherland, 2017). Lynching, for example, was an all-too-common part of American life, but the accounts of these terrorist actions against Black Americans are frequently absent from the archive. Sutherland explains that this erasure does further violence to Black Americans, removing any accountability from the perpetrators and the state that was complicit in these crimes. This erasure harms Black Americans and changes a core part of U.S. history. As Florini writes, "In U.S. culture, historicizing an event often serves to depoliticize it and works to produce consensus. Thus, controversial or contradictory accounts of the past are often erased or marginalized in the service of historicizing racism, relegating it to the past, and therefore facilitating contemporary disavowal of its existence" (Florini, 2014, p. 317). Black women were core users and creators of technology during the antebellum period in the U.S. but remain mostly absent in the written record. The master narrative does not grant space to Black women's words or document Black women's creativity in changing and growing the uses and possibilities of these technologies. While historians point to plausible reasons why white women's and Black women's and men's history is harder to find in the archive, I argue that not collecting these records is an example of archival amnesty. The absence of Black women in our understanding of technology is an intentional practice of erasure doing further violence to an already oft violated group. Excluding Black women from the history of technology furthers the now sedimented idea that white men are most responsible for technological innovation.

So how does one go about documenting Black women's relationship to labor and technology without relying on her enslaver to do the telling? The task of tracking the everyday experience of women in history is extraordinarily challenging. Social historians typically use sites like "city directories, probate records, the house-by-house jotting of the census," which all but ignore women. As Lebsock explains, "Accumulating evidence about ordinary men is never painless or quick; tracking women is more difficult still" (Lebsock, 1985, p. xiv). If we extend this to the task of tracking Black women, the challenge becomes seemingly impossible. The scarcity of documentation is a symptom of a more significant ailment, which is society's unwillingness to see Black women in their full humanity. Despite the circumstances, Black women have managed to leave for themselves a record of survival. In their own words, Black women are full and complex emotional and technologically adept human beings. Without their words to guide us, we must read Black women in the gaps and spaces of the archives of the early Americas. When enslavers recorded a new life in the family bible, we can locate Black women as wet nurses. In the records of enslaved Africans passed on to children as property in wills, Black women whose children were sold away by tyrants remain in the shadow.[2] History may overlook Black women's ingenuity in crafting efficient household technologies, but their tools remain.[3] Because the U.S. has used Black women as engines of labor, the products of that labor are a part of the dominant narrative and are accessible in the archive. From these labor records, we can extract pieces of the fullness of their lived experiences.

## Ain't I a Laborer?

Black women's role as laborers has complicated their relationship with societal constructs of femininity. While we now know she was intentionally misquoted,[4] Sojourner Truth's "Ain't I a Woman" speech delivered in Akron, Ohio, in 1851 makes a case for Black women's suffrage and rights to an audience reticent to see Black women as *real* women.[5] The speech given by Truth displays her rhetorical and oratorical skills. Truth situates Black womanhood as distinct from white womanhood based on the hardships and injustices that Black women endure. Likewise, she explains that Black women were working as long and as hard as men, which in no way separates Black women from their womanhood. If anything, it complicates and expands notions of womanhood. In this pronouncement, Truth unsettles ideas of "women's work," reminding us that as white women feminists fought for the right to work alongside men later in the twentieth century, Black women had already been there, working all along.

In the Americas, European colonizers crafted the idea of "women's work" in the late seventeenth and early eighteenth centuries from English norms. Gender in the territories that would become the U.S. initially mirrored what early slave-holding colonists experienced in Europe, leaving many patriarchal norms intact. White men expected their wives to contribute to the household through domestic labor, with white women's economic lives confined to their homes (Norton, 1984). However, many English slave-holding men also expected their wives to work in the field in addition to domestic household labor. Few enslaved Black women worked in the home or had access to domestic labor before the latter part of the eighteenth century. In the early seventeenth century, in places like the Virginia colony, tobacco farming was so intensely profitable that the labor of enslaved Black men and women went to this end (Shammas, 1985). Even enslaved Black women who nursed and tended children were also field-workers (White, 1999).

In the retelling of our history, some imagine the labor of enslaved people of African descent as men's work. While scholars too often ignore the labor of Black women, Lerner describes, "The lot of Black women under slavery was in every respect more arduous, difficult and restricted than that of the men." It was not until later and with more wealth that planters extended the primary work of many Black enslaved women to the household (Lerner, 1973, p. 15). As the number of Black women born in the colonies increased, planters could transfer some labor from the field to craftwork and domestic labor. Without the textile industry in the colonies, spinning became a primary task for enslaved women responsible for crafting clothing for other enslaved people on the property. Even still, some estimate that only 5–15 percent of Black enslaved women were nonfield workers (Shammas, 1985). For example, the average slave-holding family in the Virginia colony kept only one to two female Black women for domestic tasks for the family and the rest of the enslaved community (Shammas, 1985). We require a new narrative of labor that recenters Black women as skilled laborers and users of agricultural, domestic, and communicative technology.

Enslavers needed to cultivate a separation between the labor and lives of white and Black women. This need drove the transition of domestic work from white women within the household to Black enslaved women. The separation of labor is a fundamental driving force in maintaining white supremacy and patriarchy, with Black women relegated to the lowest rung on the hierarchical ladder. White women could only be separated from the conditions of labor *because* they enslaved Black women as domestic laborers. Angelina Grimké Weld, an abolitionist and writer in the mid-1900s, describes white women's utter reliance on Black women's labor. Recounting the experience of a white enslaver, she explained that Juba, a Black woman, "dressed and undressed her, gave her all her food and was so necessary that [she] could not do without her" (Weld, 1839, pp. 42–45). Like so many, Juba's existence made her enslaver's life possible.

The separation of white women from labor, both in the field and in the home, helped develop the troupe of white women's fragility. Françoise Burgess writes that white women came to be "defined by the plantation ideology—her fragility, purity, chastity, and domesticity" (Burgess, 1996, p. 100). The cult of true womanhood, also referred to as the cult of domesticity,[6] created a separation between the private world of the white woman (the home) and the public world of the white man. As Carby explains, the cult of true womanhood was "a dominating image, describing the parameters within which women were measured and declared to be, or not to be, women" (Carby, 1987, p. 23). Proponents of expanding slavery across the newly formed nation used white women's fragility to make their case. Fragility necessitated white women's protection from Black men and that Black women's labor was needed to maintain a proper household and a comfortable white family life. This trope of white femininity ultimately protects white supremacist patriarchy. Yet white women had to accept this characterization as fragile and in need of protection for this ideological construct to work. White women consented to a construction of their womanhood made possible only in contrast to Black women. As keepers of white women's homes, while enslaved, and later as income earners in a "free" economy, Black women's lives could not fit within the conventions of the cult of true womanhood. Black women spent their time shifting between the care of their own families and their work as laborers. Being a Black woman during and postslavery required the ability to shift between norms, occupy each expertly, and hide that expertise to prevent unwanted attention, which would result in further exploitation or violence.

The separation between the worlds of the white woman and Black women is part of a larger project of white supremacy born of a desire to protect a dwindling majority for whites in states increasingly filled with enslaved Black people. States measured their population by measuring white men's population against the entire Black population, including enslaved men and women (Wood, 1996). White supremacist patriarchy necessitated they did not conflate white men's and white women's social, legal, and economic states. The cult of true womanhood, which intertwines patriarchy and white supremacy in the advancement of U.S. capitalism, dictated that white womanhood was found acceptable or lacking by its proximal distance to manhood. But within this same convoluted system, Black women were counted and treated as property no different from Black men. Politically and economically, it was essential to mark the distinctions between white men and women but not between Black men and women. Conflating Black men and women is beneficial to the project of white supremacy and capitalist enterprise. As Spillers explains, "The female body and the male body become a territory of cultural and political maneuver" (Spillers, 1987, p. 67). Counted alongside Black men and precluded from idealized notions of womanhood and femininity, Black women's technical expertise in both the home and the field was ignored.

Black women worked alongside Black men cultivating crops and using agricultural innovation to propel America's wealth forward. Enslaved Black men and women were trained artisans, craftsmen, seamstresses, cooks, and cultivators of goods for sale in marketplaces. Their technical skill in agriculture generated a thriving tobacco industry in South Carolina. Their technical knowledge of planting and harvesting was essential on rice fields in the Carolinas and Virginia. Wood (1996) counters the description of enslaved Black persons as "unskilled labor." He explains, "It seems safe to venture that if Africans had shown much less competence in, or aptitude for, such basic frontier sills as managing boats, clearing land, herding cattle, working wood, and cultivating fields, their importation would not have continued to grow. . . . It is worthwhile to suggest here that with respect to rice cultivation, particular know-how, rather than lack of it, was one factor that which made Black labor attractive to the English colonists" (Wood, 1996, p. 65). Black women's technical expertise in Black domestic labor through work like canning and sewing and their culinary skill and medical knowledge made some plantations self-sustaining. Black women worked efficiently and with no acknowledgment. Their work, often invisible, and their mastery of the field and home technologies made the life of the white plantation-owning family possible and gave life to a new generation of American-born persons of African descent.

## Technology Is Not for Ladies

Enslavers commonly sold Black women as "fit for the field or house" (Wood, 1996, p. 313). This venomous description unwittingly speaks to Black women's mastery of multiple forms of labor and the ability to move fluidly between vastly different environments. Black women's work in homes and the fields required varied communicative and social practice. But as technology became synonymous with expertise, efficiency, and skill, it became attached to white masculinity and divorced from Black women's personhood. To justify enslavement, white citizens worked to separate the idea of technical skills from slave labor. With the invocation of the cult of true womanhood, white women became removed from the labor force and, therefore, from American ideals of efficiency, productivity, and technology. However, the American economic system required Black women to be a part of the labor force and, therefore, engines of technology and efficiency.

Black women have always engaged with technology; it is the definition of technology and technical expertise that shifted. Black women, as purveyors of the home, had to master many forms of technology. However, if the everyday use of the term *technology* shifts to no longer include their tools, systems of labor, and modes of communication, their labor, bodies, and expertise could be devalued. This idea persists today in beliefs and policies that view the labor done by Black and brown persons, white women, and low-income earners as unskilled work, worthy of less pay, fewer benefits, and less respect. Society has separated ideas of home from work, "unskilled" from "skilled" labor, domesticity from technology, and eventually blue- and pink-collar from white-collar work.

The willful and intentional erasure of Black women as whole agentic technophiles from our collective memory does essential work for white supremacy. Rather than situating Black women as agentic beings with technical skills, Collins (2009) explains that white society viewed Black women using controlling images like mammies and jezebels. The stereotypes and tropes that exist for Black women are based on the relationship of white society to her body. Mammies' bodies produced nourishment for white children and families. Their frames, full and soft, provided comfort and rest for white babies. Their bodies were not for their use, and their minds were not given consideration. A "jezebel's" body was a threat to white women and families. Their frames, desirable and sensual, proved a useful counter to white women's perceived gentleness and purity. Again, the minds of Black women warranted no regard.

There are material consequences to the use and deployment of these tropes. People harm the bodies of, ignore the desires of, and violate the personage of Black women. New tropes like the Strong Black Woman (Morgan, 2000) laud Black women for their resilience while providing cover for lower pay, lack of resources, and sexual and physical violence.[7] Black women are still not seen as fully human with the capacity for rich emotional and social lives and possessing desires and dreams. Dominant U.S. society does not treat Black women as though we feel harm, pain, joy, or contentment. Therefore, society feels entitled to use us, drain us, and move on without care. The Black woman's body—rather than her cunning, skill, and ingenuity—has become her only useful contribution to American life. Yet Black women's bodies do not exist separately from the mind. Even in the deplorable stereotypes meant to mock and marginalize Black women, the mammy and jezebel demonstrate the full capacity of Black women. Black women were caretakers who ran households, crafted medicinal cures for ailments, delivered babies, fashioned devices used to feed, clothe, and provide sustenance to their own families and families in their care. Black women were also sexual beings whose agency was often ripped from them even as they used their cunning to survive the most egregiously violent of circumstances. These tropes remove Black women from their rightful place as craftspersons, skilled workers of the land, household and domestic technicians, and communicative experts.

The media still frames Black women and girls as absent from the world of technology. With headlines like "Why Do Girls Lose Interest in STEM?" (Choney, 2018) or "Women, Minorities Continually Left Behind" (D'Onofrio, 2015), we are missing the opportunity to interrogate Black women's systematic exclusion for its racist origins. These headlines and others like them blame Black women for their absence in the tech industry, situate the (supposed) absence as a choice, or offer solutions through increased recruitment. However, Black women did not get left behind in the tech industry; instead, the tech industry has not treated Black women's technological expertise as real or valuable. Efforts like Black Girls CODE are reasonable attempts to correct for underrepresentation. However, the emphasis on coding as a measure of technical skill keeps the racist and sexist usage of the word *technology* intact. Indeed, Black women and girls who do not code still have a tremendous amount of knowledge about how technologies work, are deployed, and can be reimagined.

While I question the use and deployment of the term *technology* in its current form, I do not suggest we view technology solely as a tool of oppression. Amiri Baraka (1969) suggests that Black folks' encounter with the U.S. since the transatlantic slave trade has been a history bound up with their encounters with Western technology. These encounters with technology have, he argues, been the source of our oppression. From the slave ship to the shackle and the cotton gin, technologies of oppression held Africans captive on American soil. Captors fashioned more efficient and effective technologies to keep Black people in captivity as the labor source. Citing Walton (1999), Fouché writes, "Technology such as the ships that transported African slaves to the 'New World,' the overseers' whips, cotton cultivation, 'Jim Crow' rail cars, segregated buses, inner-city public housing, and voting machines have contributed, directly or indirectly, to the subjugation of African American people" (Fouché, 2006, p. 640). According to Baraka (1969), Western technology was created for and alongside systemic oppression, and therefore freedom must be freedom from Western technology.

However, as I have outlined thus far, Black women are not inept at the use and creation of technology, nor has our encounter with technology been confined to using tools created by white slave owners. Instead, as Fouché posits, technology as material oppression is not the only way to consider African American technological experiences. As interesting as this mode of analysis can be for thinking about the technological control of African Americans, it strips Black people of technological agency. It inherently closes down discussions about the ways African American people consume and use technology and conceals the reasons that Black people produce meanings for technological artifacts, practices, and knowledge that regularly subvert the architectured, or constructed, meanings of technology. A major limitation of this perspective is that it does not embrace the ways that African American people acquire technological agency by being resourceful, innovative, and most important, creative. (Fouché, 2006, p. 640)

Fouché calls this "survival technology." In many cases, perception of what "counts" as a technological activity "is deeply intertwined with deleterious representations of the racialized other. In other words, technological activities that cannot be effectively categorized within the dominant canon of science and technology fall to the wayside" (Fouché, 2006, p. 642).

## Master's Tools

Thus far, I have positioned Black women as creators, purveyors, and innovators of technologies of domestic and agricultural labor. Beyond the manipulation of physical technology, Black women used rhetorical and communicative devices as tools to dismantle oppression, transforming the voice into a technology of survival and resistance. As the U.S. weaponized access to education to delay Black folks' autonomy and freedom, enslaved Africans continued to pursue literacy. While acquiring reading and writing skills, Black Americans maintained a counterculture deeply connected to orality. The preservation of oral culture[8] in the U.S. provided Black Americans a new language and dialect[9] by combining West African traditions with white Western Americanized English. Orality also yielded a rhetorical tradition that used the voice as a survival technology. The collective voice of Black folks has been among the community's most durable and useful technologies.

From the antebellum South to the present, Americans of African descent used oral traditions to create and conceive of community, resist oppression, and practice the public expression of joy (Lu & Steele, 2019). Black oral traditions like folktales and playing the dozens demonstrate the cleverness of Black American language. Henry Louis Gates Jr. (2014) documents the origins of signifyin'[10] to West African tradition and the particularities of the experiences of those held in bondage in the Americas. This creative linguistic technique showcases at once the determination to keep Black diasporic culture intact and the necessity to form new patterns of communication based on experiences of oppression. The ability to hide meanings and produce possibilities to sort out conflict and joy in full view of one's oppressor is a feature of the Black rhetorical tradition. Black women learned to wield the power of their voice to hide meaning from both white folks and Black men.

Based on their distance from whiteness but proximity to masculinity, Black men's discursive patterns may too often approximate the objectives of white men—to wield power and assert dominance. If Black men use their rhetorical skills to pursue racial justice while leaving patriarchy intact, the voice is not truly a technology of freedom. Toxic and hegemonic forms of masculinity require men, both Black and white, to place as much distance as possible between the skills, behaviors, and norms of themselves and those identified as women. Black men's potential to benefit from patriarchy can render Black women an obstacle in crafting their rhetorical arguments for freedom. Alternately, Black feminist rhetorical skill and technological skill are derived from multiple oppressions and wielded to dismantle multiple systems of power simultaneously. As Black feminist activist Brittany Packnett Cunningham asserts, we as Black women "have two hands: one is to battle, one is to build" (Packnett, 2017).[11] Using Black oral traditions, Black feminists have transformed the voice into a revolutionary survival technology of resistance and healing.

In 1979, Black feminist writer and activist Audre Lorde said, "For the master's tools will never dismantle the master's house. They may allow us temporarily to beat him at his own game, but they will never enable us to bring about genuine change" (Lorde, 2007, p. 112). In this speech, Lorde makes the case that we are lost if our only mechanism for *examining* an unjust system is through the tools provided by that system. To examine the racist, sexist, classist, and imperialist history and deployment of Western technology, we cannot use the same tools used to create it to critique it. However, the history of Black women's use of technology shows that "Western" technology exists because of kidnapped Africans' labor and ingenuity. White Western technology has developed based in part on the relationship of Black women to it. The tools of digital technology do not belong exclusively to the "master." Regardless of the intention of specific technologies to subjugate, Black women have long found chasms within which to undermine the logic of this system of oppression and craft space to survive and thrive. In the chapters that follow, I discuss how Black women create and deploy survival technology in digital spaces. I then provide a new mechanism for examining those spaces—one that does not rely on the "tools of the master." However, before manipulating digital platforms and online sites, Black feminists postenslavement brilliantly used legal structures like marriage and social codes of respectability meant to subjugate them to break down pillars of the master's house using the "master's tools."

## "Race Women" and Resistance

Black women used their collective voices during the period of Reconstruction as tools of resistance. They crafted rhetorical arguments for freedom and drew upon respectability as a strategy—effectively using the "master's tools" to resist dehumanization. Evelyn Brooks Higginbotham describes respectability as a strategy through which Black women aimed to "earn their people a measure of esteem from white America" (Higginbotham, 1993, p. 26). In 2020, television pundits and political figures wield respectability politics to critique the Movement for Black Lives, uprisings across the country against police brutality, and Black women's reclamation of sexual agency. As a rhetorical strategy in the late nineteenth and early twentieth centuries, Black women used arguments of respectability to cut through the racist and sexist idea that Black women were not *real* women. The cult of true womanhood still firmly intact, Black women publicly performed respectability to dismantle the dominant form of racial bias. Rather than immediately seeking to break gendered norms apart, Black women first created a public mechanism to dismantle the argument that womanhood was inclusive of whites only. Black women who adopted respectability as a political strategy worked to unsettle the representation of Black folks as animals, not worthy of their newly fought-for freedom.

In the context of the burgeoning democracy, legal marital binds became a symbol of citizenship and acculturation into life as free persons. Too often in the U.S., becoming a citizen is viewed as synonymous with being *deserving* of full human rights.[12] For enslaved Africans living in the U.S., the law withheld the possibility of engaging fully with citizenship, creating legal binds through marriage, and therefore establishing themselves as deserving of their full rights. After emancipation, women sought out husbands who had been sold away, while others found themselves in the challenging predicament of having more than one husband, though neither union was legally binding. Recognizing the import placed on legal marriage, free Black women used legal marriage both to construct legally bound familial groups and as a way to achieve "respectability" and attain new freedoms.

Heteronormative marriage within a hegemonic patriarchal system places boundaries and burdens on the lives of women. However, for some Black women in the 1800s and 1900s, marriage created possibilities to function with more independence, build capital, and develop additional technological skills. Because laws denied rights to single women, marriage was the only mechanism available to some women to own land or travel. For example, Dorothy Sterling (1997) details the life of a free Black woman in the early 1800s in New England named Nancy who married a man from St. Petersburg. Upon returning to St. Petersburg with him, Nancy learned Russian in a few months and started a garment business selling children's clothes. Sterling explains that the cold winters forced Nancy home, where, apart from her husband, she became involved in "American reform movements while traveling, lecturing, teaching and writing" (Sterling, 1997, p. 95). Nancy's experience tells one story of possibility for Black women who utilized marriage as a mechanism of escape. Nancy and many other Black women in this era would not be permitted to travel in certain social or political circles but for their attachment to men. Women like Nancy used marriage to achieve financial success and to engage in political and social organizations through which they could advocate for change.

Many other free Black women recognized the need to cultivate separate lives from their husbands by forming literary societies. The Female Literary Association of Philadelphia and the African American Female Intelligence Society of Boston both operated, at least in part, to advance the notion of the respectable Black woman. Formed in 1831, the Female Literary Association of Philadelphia described its missions as follows: "As daughters of a despised race, it becomes a duty . . . to cultivate the talents entrusted to our keeping, that by doing so, we may break down the strong barriers of prejudice" (Sterling, 1997, p. 110). Black women's literary societies, unlike their male counterparts', did not often hold public events, instead choosing to meet in each other's homes and creating forums whereby they could share their writing (Dudley, 2013). However, private meetings are not synonymous with private concerns. The women regularly engaged in public issues. Elizabeth Jennings, a member of the Ladies Literary Society of New York, wrote about the importance of the mind in demonstrating Black persons' full humanity. She says, "The mind is the greatest, and great care should be taken to improve it with diligence. Neglect will plunge us into deep degradation and keep us groveling in the dust while our enemies will rejoice and say, we do not believe they (colored people) have any minds" (Sterling, 1997). She implored the women to fight back against this indignity as a service to themselves and their race. Women understood that legal and social codes would only permit their gatherings if society deemed them "respectable" married women. Black women, restricted in their method of political organization, manipulated notions like patriarchal marriage laws. They created spaces like literary societies and church groups for economic and social advancement within the bounds of an oppressive system.

Respectability politics in the late 1800 and early 1900s were a reclamation of agency and a form of protest. Black women's use of respectability, a concept created to restrict their autonomy, "reflected more than simply bourgeois Victorian ideology; it was a foundation of African American women's survival strategies and self-definition irrespective of class" (Wolcott, 2001, p. 7). As Wolcott explains, "Female activists such as Fannie Barrier Williams, Anna Julia Cooper, and Nannie Helen Burroughs wrote copiously in African American periodicals and lectured nationwide, arguing that issues of particular relevance to African American women . . . should be central to racial reform. Through their writing and activism, these women propagated an ideology of racial uplift that focused on the unique role women would play in racial advancement" (Wolcott, 2001, p. 6). Today, this strategy is still in use by digital Black feminists who craft arguments online that upon first glance, do not seem disruptive but undermine the systems erected to subjugate them.[13]

Black feminist writers and speakers had to simultaneously "prove" the humanity of African Americans and, through their performance of femininity, argue for their womanness as well. Yet many Black women decided to focus their energy and rhetorical skills on asserting the rights of Black men. Describing life in a post–Civil War America, Tera Hunter explains, Black women "faced the choice between exercising personal freedom, which emancipation offered for the first time, and acting in the interest of the collective, which their life conditions had always demanded" (Hunter, 2017, p. 40). Black women worked for the collective good and elevated their voices when they typically would be ignored.

As Brittney Cooper writes, these race women "fashioned themselves a public duty to serve their people through diligent and careful intellectual work and attention to proving the intellectual character of the race" (B. C. Cooper, 2017, p. 11). In their public speech and writings, Black women of the early twentieth century used the systems and institutions that were a binding cord of their oppression to refashion a garment of progress. "Race women" (B. C. Cooper, 2017) used the bounds and expectations of patriarchy to hone arguments for Black liberation. Many feminists regard institutions like heterosexual marriage as restrictive to women's agency. Nevertheless, they enabled the creation of Black women's enclaves wherein rhetorical skills became a technology of their freedom. The politics of respectability began as a Victorian ideal meant to shun Black women. However, respectability politics provided Black women an avenue to hone argumentation skills and cement their position in Black cultural life. Because the U.S. systematically kept Black women from literacy, property ownership, voting rights, agency over their bodies, use of their language, and free travel, they have encountered a position in this country where this kind of ingenuity and creativity are necessary for survival.

Black women's voices and feminized patterns of communication differ from Black men's in meaningful ways. Black women's voices must resist oppression based on both gender and race. In so doing, the ability to switch between objectives and audiences provides Black women a careful understanding of the interworking of both patriarchy and white supremacy. Toni Cade Bambara asserts, "We have a very particular vantage point, and, therefore, have a special contribution to make to the collective intelligence" (C. Tate, 1983, p. 14). Audre Lorde describes that vantage point as "having survived catastrophe with style" (C. Tate, 1983). Examples of the Black feminist voice as a technology of survival emerge from poets, activists, writers, and scholars from the sixteenth to the twenty-first century. Black feminist voice, crafted by Black women, is derived from the specific condition of Black women. At every turn, and in every era, Black feminist voice is constructed in proximity to Black men and white women but born out of different needs, with different cadence and urgency.

Thus far, I have focused on the experiences of Black women long before the digital turn. We began by considering the lived experiences of Black women and the boundaries erected to prevent their advancement. It is from these sites of oppression that Black women's survival and thriving use of technology emerge. Black women have developed a cadre of tools and technologies to resist domination. As Black women demonstrated mastery of skills—which required deftness, wit, and efficiency in agriculture, domestic work, artisan enterprise, and service work—America continued to devalue their labor. As Black women merged feminized modes of communication with African diasporic traditions of orality, this complex rhetorical structure was labeled deficient. The emergent definition of technology systematically removed Black women's labor and communication patterns.

Black women's relationship to labor and technology is a story of using tools and technologies crafted to oppress as mechanisms of resistance. This chapter provides us three critical lessons about this relationship. First, the digital is an extension of past mediums, a site for cultural production, and a tool of Black feminist freedom building. Therefore, we must position technologies of the voice and body alongside machinery and equipment. Second, Black womanhood has always been profitable for someone. As we turn our attention to digital production and technoculture in the chapters that follow, digital Black feminism raises essential questions about how Black women's labor and thought work can now be profitable for Black women. Finally, to understand and central-ize Black women in the study of digital tools and culture, we require a new analytical tool that breaks free from the limitations of technology as a product of whiteness. We need a device for understanding Black feminist technoculture oriented toward Black women, not white folks or Black men.

## 2

## Black Feminist Technoculture, or *the Virtual Beauty Shop*

On July 3, 2020, Black women took to Twitter to celebrate their hair. The hashtag #CROWNDay marked the anniversary of the first state law prohibiting discrimination based on hair. One year earlier, California passed the CROWN Act, which "prohibits discrimination based on hairstyles by extending statutory protections based on race to hair texture and protective styles in state Employment, Housing, Education Codes" (CROWN Act, n.d.). Since that time, additional states have passed versions of the CROWN Act. As Black women posted pictures of themselves with locs, twists, and braids and celebrated the legal victory, many also reflected on the discrimination they had faced because of their hair. Others lamented that not until 2019 had any state or the federal government passed legislation to combat this discrimination that is all too common for Black folks in schools and the workplace.

For the Black community and specifically for Black women, hair has been a source of joy and communal belonging and a site for discrimination and violence. Black women in the U.S. and across the diaspora have long taken great pride in their "crowns." European kidnappers recognized the connection Black women had to their hair and shaved the heads of captured African women to crush their dignity and separate them from their culture (Byrd & Tharps, 2014). Once in the U.S., enslaved Black women found ways to maintain their hair using techniques from home, like braiding. Postenslavement, Black women were judged by Eurocentric standards of beauty and professionalism and developed techniques for straightening hair and installation of extensions and weaves. The natural hair movement provided a new space for discussion, new sites of sharing, and new possibilities for Black women's ownership of their hair stories. Natural hair blogs provided a place where Black women could curate content and form communities of support. Black women used online platforms to share their hair journeys, post pictures of their "big chop,"[1] and share products and techniques to grow and maintain their hair. It was natural hair bloggers like Leila Noelliste (Black Girl with Long Hair) and Patrice Yursik (AfroBella) who provided my introduction to the Black blogosphere.

I spent the better part of my graduate studies researching Black discourse online. Much of what I was reading in my personal time and what I wanted to write in my research was happening on blog sites run by Black women. However, when writing my dissertation, I settled on "The Digital Barbershop" as my title and focus. The barbershop provided a useful metaphor for how blogging replicated oral culture online, the kinds of alternate publics I was studying, and how researchers ignored Black cultural sites. I used the term *barbershop* in the title to have my work read as substantive and to indicate broad trends regarding Black culture online. However, this title obscured the importance of what happened in spaces crafted by and for women and nonbinary folks. The barbershop does not always resonate as a collective space of welcome for those who are not cis men. As I sat looking at that title, I felt a deep sense of betrayal to the Black women whose work inspired my research. The beauty shop, I thought, was just as significant as the barbershop, and the barbershop was not, as I tried to make it be, a stand-in for all Black folks.

In this chapter, I introduce the metaphor of the beauty shop as an analytical tool to understand the relationship between Black women and technology and a metaphor to introduce Black feminist technoculture. While Black barbershops function as hush harbors (Nunley, 2011), or safe places for free expression among African American speakers, and counterpublics (Squires, 2002), providing insight into Black discourse online, the beauty shop provides a lens to see Black women owners, creators, and builders of platforms and spaces and a way to discuss the principles, praxes, and products of digital Black feminism. Black feminist technoculture, as seen through the beauty shop, presents a way to sever the cord from the white supremacist and patriarchal origins of the technology we study and use every day.

## Barbershops and Beauty Shops

During slavery and in the antebellum South, Black men who worked as barbers did not serve Black customers. Following emancipation, those who were trained as barbers exclusively served a white clientele and in some cases refused to allow other African Americans into the shop (Bristol, 2009). This decision was necessary to keep their white customers comfortable in a segregated Jim Crow South. White patrons flocked to Black barbershops to continue to be served by Black men postslavery (Berlin, 1974; Mills, 2014). Black barbers, therefore, had to negotiate public and private selves, maintaining separate identities at home and in the workplace to attain financial independence. In the late 1800s and early 1900s, the all-white Journeymen Barbers' International Union of America launched a series of campaigns against Black barbershops, suggesting they were unsanitary and unhygienic. In an attempt to oust Black barbers from the profession, the union's campaign dissuaded white patronage of Black barbers who were not unionized. The campaign effectively drove a wedge between the barbers, who could not afford the latest sterilization equipment, and their white customers (Bristol, 2009, p. 163). Black barbers took their professional skills and moved their shops to Black neighborhoods, carrying with them financial independence. The Black barbershop, which was once a space reserved for white men, became an alternate public within the African American community.[2] By 1920, over 200 Black barbershops were in operation in Chicago, along with 108 beauty salons catering to a Black clientele (Byrd & Tharps, 2014). Black barbers began to focus on the unique needs of Black hair care. In these shops, Black working- and middle-class male patrons received services for their hair while engaging in the rituals of Black hair care and everyday talk.

As a space hidden from the dominant gaze, the Black barbershop became a historical site of cultural importance for the Black community. Because of their professional training, Black men who worked as barbers had access to leadership roles in churches, fraternities, and other Black organizations involved in abolition movements (Mills, 2014). Even while serving a white clientele, some barbers in the 1800s used their social and financial success for social justice and community uplift. Peter Howard, a Black barber in Baltimore, used his shop as a stop on the Underground Railroad. John Smith, another Black barber in Baltimore, hosted political forums in his shop (Bristol, 2009). The barbershop signifies the cultural tradition of crafting community identities and asserting a challenge to the dominant narratives about African American men that permeate American culture. Scholars have rightly pointed to barbershops as fostering economic stability for small business owners and pride for customers and as sites of cultural reproduction. The shop has been the setting for films and television shows. But it was also a space where gender separation was apparent. The barbershop was a male-dominated space where hegemonic masculinity often prevailed, and women were excluded from meaningful participation and instead treated as subjects of discourse (C. W. Franklin, 1985).

No less skilled than their male counterparts, Black beauty shop owners served a cultural need in the community, but they have not received the same scholarly and public attention as the barbershop. As was the case for male proprietors of the barbershop, the hair care industry has provided a means of economic mobility for Black women. The first Black female millionaire, Madam C. J. Walker, made her fortune by creating a line of hair care products and tools for Black women. She helped other Black women open salons and trained what she referred to as "hair culturists" (Colman, 1994). Within this enclave, features of the beauty shop—including Black hair care technologies, entrepreneurship, the building of clienteles—all signify how Black feminist technoculture predates the social media era.

## Technologies of the Shop

In this text, I do not aim to offer a history of Black hair that scholars of Black women's history and culture have already written. Instead, I introduce the beauty shop as a metaphor for the capacities of Black feminist technoculture. The beauty shop helps us reconsider what counts as a technology by showcasing Black women's hair care technologies. The technologies of Black hair care are specific to Black people. The complicated and time-consuming task of hair grooming includes washing, combing, oiling, braiding, twisting, and decorating the hair with any number of adornments, including cloth, beads, and shells. These activities happen over many hours, sometimes even multiple days (Byrd & Tharps, 2014; Patton, 2006), requiring a commitment to both the process and the people involved. While hairstyles can be mimicked, appropriated, or appreciated by others, technologies like West African hair braiding are a cultural legacy. Black men began barbershops with white men as their clientele, but Black women created the Black beauty shop for themselves. Black women's hair care technologists created a road map for using tools to center Black women and achieve financial independence. The beauty shop's technologies are a part of a Black feminist technoculture that begins before the digital era but explains much of Black women's mastery of said era. The beauty shop displays Black hair care technologies' brilliance, the entrepreneurship of Black women proprietors of the shop, and Black feminist communication strategies. In each of these ways, digital culture capitalizes on these technologies of "the shop."

*Hair Care*

Black technologies of hair care began before chattel slavery in America, but as Patton (2006) argues, slavery changed Black folks' relationship to their hair. In the Americas, Black hair, like Blackness, was deemed unacceptable and inferior. Hiding one's hair became both socially and legally regulated through tignon laws.[3] Yet Black women found creative ways to care for their hair. Following the Civil War, Black women mastered hair technologies to change their natural texture to mirror the dominant group more closely. Straightening one's hair was a survival technology rooted in respectability (Byrd & Tharps, 2014). While chemical processing and straightening receive critique for their origins in white supremacy, Black women's use of these technologies demonstrates the ability to invent and create hair care strategies that provide safety and employment possibilities. Hair straightening and weave and wig installations also demonstrate the ability to find profit and benefit within the system of one's oppression. Beyond these styles, Black women also held on to other hair care technologies from West Africa, like braiding.

In the last decade, white celebrities and mainstream fashion magazines have *discovered* braids. Celebrities like Kim Kardashian and white influencers around the globe participate in an appropriation of Black culture and aesthetics. They have formed careers by making what has been deemed unkempt, unacceptable, and unprofessional on Black women palatable for a white audience. Even as braids have gained popularity among communities outside of the Black experience, Black women and girls are still routinely punished for wearing braids.

In 2017, Maya and Deanna Cook, sophomores at a charter school just outside of Boston, were kicked off their sports teams and banned from prom because, as the school explained, their braids violated a policy against "wearing their hair in an unnatural way" (J. Williams, 2017). An eleven-year-old girl in Louisiana was sent home from school after being told her shoulder-length braided ponytail was "unacceptable" (Rosenblatt, 2018). Even dancers in the Harlem production of *Black Nutcracker* were banned from the show in 2019 because they elected to keep their hair in braids (Thornton, 2019). Braids for Black hair serve as a protective style, keeping the hair free from excessive pulling or tangling, frictional breakage, and harsh heat or chemical treatments. Braids have also historically served as means of identity and community cohesion (Collier, 2006; Dixon, 2005; Johnson, 2011). Andréa Rose Clarke explains braiding as a technology with a rule structure like that of an algorithm. Clarke says,

> Design and fabrication tools perform aesthetic gestures based preset commands and algorithms. The execution and repetition of a series procedures produces the patterns we see as braids. It is this closed system of rules that allows for variable patterns to evolve. In a manner akin to the precision of a laser cutter burning and etching image into material the braider maps and parts the hair in preparation for plaiting a series of cornrows. The sectioning of the hair is done with mathematical understanding. Speed and efficiency are also criteria that a braider will be judged by. Sophisticated calculations occur at multiple points of a braiding session. These almost instantaneously and seemingly intuitive decisions allow for even distribution of braids across the three-dimensional surface of the head. (Clarke, 2018, para. 2)

Clarke asks us to consider how braids happen rather than focusing on braids as the end product. Braiding requires sophisticated design decisions and technical expertise. As Nettrice Gaskins (2014) explains, "Certain patterns are amenable or open to algorithmic modeling—but 'amenable' need not connote the simple—a square is easier to simulate and repeat but the process of braiding, knitting or weaving these shapes into designs is more about complexity arising from simplicity. In other words, it is not the braid itself but the act of interweaving shapes that form the intricate patterns that unify the design" (para. 15). Whether braids are covered by a wig or weave, are adorned with beads, or feature intricate patterns on full display, they are a collective project wherein the braider's skill, efficiency, and aesthetic design meet the imagination and scalp of her partner. The beautician's own complex system of codes, braiding is a mathematical and artistic design experience. The symbiotic relationship between the braider and the braidee requires hours spent together and shared objectives—a codependency. In this relationship, technology flourishes without adherence to white Western values like individualism. Braids are not only an artifact of Black cultural production; they are a way to understand *how* Black technoculture culture comes to be.

## Entrepreneurs

In the beauty shop, skilled beauticians train and perfect the implementation of these technologies. In addition to traditional businesses, Black women created hair salons in their homes, servicing neighbors, their church communities, and extended families. As Tiffany Gill explains, "The antebellum period saw the emergence of successful black female hairdressers, women who turned hairdressing from a servant's obligation to a business enterprise" (Gill, 2010, p. 10). The *how* of the shop also tells a story of exclusion from the traditional economy and entrepreneurship. While not considered in the long history of small business success stories, "Black women have sustained a commercial and cultural tradition of self-help that has distinguished the economic lives of Black women in America for almost 400 years" (C. A. Smith, 2005). Black women are often ignored because the mechanisms by which success is measured, including the size of business and profits, are less applicable to these business owners (C. A. Smith, 2005). Smith calls these women "lifestyle entrepreneurs."

Black women's beauty shops—with their small but loyal clientele, whom they serviced in their homes rather than at a formal establishment—paved the way for lifestyle entrepreneurs and the near ubiquity of today's influencer culture.[4] Black women's entrepreneurship in the beauty shop thrives within a system that does not equally disperse loans, provide capital, offer formal business training, or provide education in marketing and development. Black beauty shop owners master marketing and branding often without formal training and within an enclave where they rely on other Black women for support. Black patrons of beauty shops are notoriously loyal to their beauticians (Harris-Lacewell, 2010). The beautician's technical skill set and personality, aesthetics of the shop, communication dynamics within the shop, and services available to patrons differentiate one shop from another. Generating business, followers, or readers online is also akin to beauticians' crafting of a loyal clientele.

Transferring these skills to online platforms, lifestyle bloggers, social media entrepreneurs, and influencers develop loyal followings through carefully curated interaction, responding directly to readers in the comments section or creating an alternate means to contact them and seek their advice and guidance (Steele, 2018). They may also build rapport using shared cultural experiences, language, and influences. Social media entrepreneurs create a high context for participation. Followers are positioned as insiders and are more likely to remain loyal to the blog, page, or account when they possess the background needed to continue participating. Like the beauty shop owners who first understood this essential skill, lifestyle entrepreneurs often do not have a physical location for their business. They therefore engage in nontraditional mechanisms for marketing to their clientele. Mastering the now lucrative technology of marketing and branding oneself in the growing field of lifestyle entrepreneurship and influencer culture is forged from a long history of exclusion from the traditional economy. Bloggers, influencers, and lifestyle entrepreneurs are responsible for establishing the thematic content, tone/tenor of discourse, and the site/page's architecture that evokes participation and engagement from the reader/follower. As "shop owners," bloggers are the proprietors of their establishments and regulate their activities while benefitting financially from the blog's success. Black beauty shops, just like Black women's blogs, form from a long legacy of entrepreneurship and branding.

*Shoptalk*

Black feminist technoculture develops in spaces wherein Black women and nonbinary folks find safe harbor. The unique nature of Black hair care and the dialogue that surrounds the practice make hairstyling an "in-group activity" (Harris-Lacewell, 2010). Early Black barbers could cater to a white clientele by keeping Black culture, linguistic patterns, and people away. Later, their shops existed as "hush harbors" (Nunley, 2011). The Black beauty shop has always been and continues to be a place of such retreat. The beauty shop functioned as an enclave, a safe space of communal sharing for Black women. Unlike counterpublics that seek engagement with the dominant group, enclaves hide counterhegemonic ideas from the dominant group for protection and survival (Squires, 2002). Outside the gaze, Black women openly discuss things personal to the community with no need to hide their opinion for fear of reprisal. The beauty shop provides a place where no one is confused by Black hair, and no explanation is required for one's hair care needs. Shoptalk fosters an appreciation of Black feminist principles for dialogue, such as personal ways of knowing, validation of emotion, personal accountability, and a preference for narrative and dialogue over debate. Within the virtual beauty shop, users replicate features of oral culture, creating more culturally specific processes of explanation and storytelling. On social network sites and in the blogosphere, there is likewise a shift away from elite notions of knowledge, definitive "correctness" in writing, and notions of traditionally conceived privacy that reflect the community-building priorities of orality more than the hierarchical priorities of literacy.[5]

Black bloggers, online lifestyle entrepreneurs, and influencers who manage and operate their sites act as the facilitators of discourse. They guide their pages' tones and themes, control content, and benefit both socially and economically from creating high-context, branded community discourse sites. The Black beauty shop's technologies financially protect and sustain Black women and their families. Just as hair care technologies create opportunities for ingenuity that support Black women's agency and identity, so too do digital spaces. In its original form and as a metaphor for Black feminist technoculture, the beauty shop unsettles the centrality of whiteness in technology.

## From the Margin to the Center

Much of the early history of digital technology and research all but erased Black folks from the internet.[6] Scholars like Anna Everett, Adam Banks, and André Brock, writing about race and Blackness online, contradicted the digital divide as the only mechanism to consider marginalized communities and the internet. They did this work with a deep and abiding commitment to Black lives. Recently, with the popularity of Black Twitter and the use of social networking sites as a mechanism to coordinate around social movements, Black internet studies have exploded. Following the visibility of hashtag activism and online social justice organizing in the 2010s, Black folks' use of social media and digital technology is no longer easily ignored or studied as an anomaly. However, research that focuses on representation or simply provides examples of Black folks' online interactions does not unsettle the flawed logic that keeps Black users on the margins in conversations about technology and technoculture. Utilizing the virtual beauty shop to push for increased coverage of or representation of Black women in news and research falls short of the possibilities of what this analytical tool can do. Likewise, research about the beauty shop's role in enforcing the adoption of white standards of beauty and colorist practices may provide context to our discussion about this framework's limitations.[7] However, such a focus removes Black women from the center of the discussion and positions Black women's actions, ideologies, and capacities within a system wherein they have no control. What happens if we instead read the beauty shop through a Black feminist lens that decentralizes Black men and white folks' importance in constructing Black women's spaces, ideas, and possibilities? The beauty shop provides a mechanism to see the rhetorical, entrepreneurial, survivalist technologies deployed for and by Black women. The beauty shop shifts our gaze and our framework for understanding Blackness, Black women, and Black technoculture.

Brock labels Black cyberculture as "digital practice and artifacts informed by a Black aesthetic" (Brock, 2020). He differentiates Black cyberculture from technoculture, defining the latter as a combination of whiteness and modern technologic beliefs. Instead, he argues that Black cyberculture arises from the aesthetic and libidinal. Black cyberculture reflects Black folks' ability to interject pleasure and joy into technology from a Black experience, too often considered solely one of pain and deprivation. Brock's critical interjection asks us to consider how Black folks' unique experiences are transposed into their relationship with technology. Brock's work provides a valuable starting point by separating Black cultural production from white cyberculture. Building upon his logic, I assert that digital Black feminism may be uniquely suited to undercut the reach and power of white (men's) cyberculture. Black women's unique experience with oppression and resistance shapes their ability to understand and utilize communication technologies, both analog and digital. If (white) technoculture is built on white ideology, patriarchy, and misogyny, Black feminist technoculture is its undoing. It also requires us to see Black women as central to Black cyberculture, not a peripheral or unnamed part. When we view Black feminist technoculture without comparison to (white) technoculture or Black (men's) cyberculture, the boxes of patriarchy and white supremacy do not constrict Black women's potential.

The beauty shop as a metaphor reminds us that Black feminism is not a reaction to white feminism; it predates it. Before white feminists fought for voting rights or the right to work,[8] Black women, as Toni Morrison writes, "had nothing to fall back on; not maleness, not whiteness, not ladyhood, not anything. And out of the profound desolation of her reality, she may well have invented herself" (Morrison, 1971, para. 19). Unlike white women suffragists who sought to prove their strength and viability in the world of men, "Black women had already proven their inherent strengths—both physical and psychological. They had undergone a baptism of fire and emerged intact" (Giddings, 1984, p. 55). Black feminism existed in the early Americas through insurgent actions of enslaved Black women who simultaneously fought white slaveholders for their freedom while caring and attending to families and asserting their agency over their bodies and minds (Giddings, 1984). Black enslaved women fought white supremacy through their love for each other and Black men (Hunter, 2017). Race women of the twentieth century crafted rhetorical campaigns that asserted their freedom (B. C. Cooper, 2017). This freedom was not rooted in a desire to wield power taken from Black men or white women. Instead, the aim of Black feminist work from early colonial America to now is revolutionary emancipatory freedom from the confines of hegemonic power divides. This differentiates Black feminism from some forms of (white) feminism that only seek parity with white men and from any type of Black nationalism that would dismantle white supremacy while leaving patriarchy intact. Black feminist thought focuses on dismantling systems of oppression rather than attempting to join them. Defining Black feminism as filling in the gaps of what white feminism leaves may be expedient for an introductory women's studies class, but it is historically inaccurate.

Whiteness is a limitation on the possibilities of both digital technology and feminism. In competition neither with white shops for business nor with hair care technologies dependent on white women, Black women created the beauty shop to suit their unique experiences, needs, and hair textures. Therefore, the virtual beauty shop is a lens to understand the possibilities of technology by moving Black women from the margins to the center. Black feminist technoculture changes the lens through which we view the possibilities, limitations, histories, and futures of digital technology. Technology, like feminism, cannot be studied as a product of whiteness. Like Black feminism, the beauty shop is a product of the imagination and labor of Black women. In the remainder of this chapter, I build the virtual beauty shop as an analytical tool by drawing on Patricia Hill Collins's "matrix of domination," Joan Morgan's "Black feminist shades of gray," and Anna Everett's "Black technophilia." Taken together, this approach to the study of Black feminist technoculture and digital Black feminism speaks to Black women's experience, resilience, and resistance and the complications of constructing Black feminism in the digital.

## Matrix of Domination and the "Gift of Loneliness"

Kimberlé Crenshaw (1990) coined the term *intersectionality* to describe how the criminal justice system was incapable of providing justice to Black women, whose oppression resided at the intersection of their race and gender. Poor Black women faced an even more massive chasm between themselves and the systems that profess blind justice to all Americans. Crenshaw's (1990) essay "Mapping the Margins" focuses on unpacking Black women's systemic oppression by examining the legal system's history and its impact on Black women's lives. Crenshaw's application to the law exposes the fundamental disconnect between

American systems of governance and Black women as American citizens meant to participate in such a system. Brittney Cooper explains that "Crenshaw's essays catalyzed a tectonic shift in the nature of feminist theorizing by suggesting that Black women's experiences demanded new paradigms in feminist theorizing, creating an analytic framework that exposed through use of a powerful metaphor exactly what it meant for systems of power to be interactive, and explicitly tying the political aims of an inclusive democracy to a theory and account of power" (B. C. Cooper, 2016, p. 2). Crenshaw's "intersectionality" is shorthand for a theory of Black women's experience, subordination, and systematic oppression that Black feminist thinkers have discussed and written about for centuries. Black feminist thinkers like Sojourner Truth, Anna Julia Cooper, Ida B. Wells-Barnett, Audre Lorde, Mary Church Terrell, the Combahee River Collective, and Deborah King had all publicly pointed to the unique vantage point of Black women and the implications of this position on their access to resources and treatment by the legal system.

As conceptualized by Black feminist thinkers like the Combahee River Collective (1983), Lorde (1984), Crenshaw (1990), and Collins (1989; Collins & Bilge, 2016), intersectionality is a tool used to understand and potentially dismantle unjust systems of legalized and socialized oppression of Black women. The term *intersectionality* signals that "oppressions work together in producing injustice" (Collins, 2009, p. 21). Recently, the use of *intersectionality* has traversed far from its original meaning. It has become a catchall term used by many new to Black feminist thought to signify multiple identities or different perspectives, to signal the inclusion of women of color, or as a descriptor of the ways that everyone has competing points of privilege (Dhamoon, 2010). As Crenshaw explained, "This is what happens when an idea travels beyond the context and the content" (Coaston, 2019). Nikol G. Alexander-Floyd (2012) describes the misuse of intersectionality as a part of a postmodern, postfeminist turn wherein Black women are disappeared and structural analysis is replaced (Tasker & Negra, 2007) with "liberal forms of inclusion" emphasizing "gender and racial representation while short-circuiting more far-reaching social and political change" (Alexander-Floyd, 2012, p. 1). Barbara Tomlinson explains, "Few theories are as consistently misrepresented" (Tomlinson, 2018, p. 3). I cannot overstate the importance of Crenshaw's theoretical work and public scholarship in bringing intersectionality to the masses. Yet even Crenshaw says she is "amazed at how [intersectionality] gets over- and under-used" (Robertson, 2017). As Ange-Marie Hancock's history of the theory warns against intersectionality becoming a meme (Hancock, 2016) and feminist scholars wrestle with the term's misuse and misunderstanding, I remain drawn to the "matrix of domination" as outlined in *Black Feminist Thought* (Collins, 2009).

The same year Crenshaw first published her essay on intersectionality, Collins described the matrix of domination as a theoretical and analytical tool to challenge a "historically specific organization of power in which social groups are embedded and which they aim to influence" (Collins, 2009, p. 246). Using the matrix of domination to interrogate Black women's experiences in the U.S., Collins explains how power is rooted in the economic, political, and social lives of Black women. The visualization of a matrix requires us to consider the environment in which oppression develops, the structure of inequality, and the complicated way these systems surround Black women. Matrices often contain multiple elements that are not immediately visible. The elements are interconnected and are reliant on each other to make meaning of the larger whole. A matrix also makes the cracks within such a system more visible. Beyond its theoretical work, there is a rhetorical utility to the phrase *matrix of domination*. "Matrix of domination" resists the appropriation, misuse, and memeification of intersectionality in popular culture. The phrase requires speakers to attend to unequal power distribution and white male supremacy.

According to Patricia Hill Collins (2009), Black women's oppression has three interdependent dimensions. First, Black women's labor has long been exploited and undervalued, which has real consequences for Black women and Black families' financial independence and economic security. The second is a political dimension that includes inequitable treatment in criminal proceedings, voter suppression, and governmental underrepresentation. Finally, Collins discusses how controlling images in the media impact our nation's ideology, underlining racist and sexist ideas through stereotypes like the mammy and jezebel. These three dimensions help us understand the implications of oppressive systems that economically, politically, and ideologically construct subordination in the U.S. However, Collins's approach to the intersecting oppressions of Black women also focuses on "reclaiming Black women's ideas" and "reinterpreting existing works through new theoretical frameworks by examining the work of Black women who are not considered intellectuals" (Collins, 2009, pp. 16–17). The matrix of domination explains how interlocking systems of oppression spur Black women's ingenuity and allow us to chart the technological and rhetorical products produced by Black women in addition to the mechanisms used to sustain systems of oppression.

Black feminist thought is a product of "oppositional knowledges" produced by Black women (Collins, 2009). Black women fashioned notions of self and community both despite and because of the oppressive forces they endured. Their labor, often happening inside the homes of white families, made them privy to worlds hidden from Black men. This "outsider-within" experience shapes Black women's relationship to power. Alice Walker writes, "The gift of loneliness is sometimes a radical vision of society or one's people that has not previously been taken into account" (O'Brien, 1973, p. 204). From this isolating perspective, Black women intellectuals create Black feminism and work to dismantle the matrix of domination using oppositional knowledge. Black feminist writers create worlds of and for Black women in their writing while excluded from the public sphere.

This "gift" of loneliness provides a unique perspective for Black women living in the U.S. Yet the solitary act of writing on paper or with a typewriter invited Black feminist thinkers to divorce their product from their practice. The process of writing itself is often a solitary venture with no possibility of immediate feedback. This means that Black feminist writers in a predigital era were working without a technological structure that supported a communal experience. We in the West have perhaps too long generated knowledge this way. We have not considered that this mechanism for generating thought can be more restrictive than liberatory. Isolation, independence, and individualism are antithetical to the praxis of Black feminism. Digital culture complicates the outsider-within construct and opens new possibilities for producing ideas in communal ways online, whereas digital affordances like immediacy create new challenges for digital Black feminists within the matrix. The matrix of domination provides a systematic way of interrogating digital technologies' impact on the production of Black feminist thought in a digital age. Collin's "matrix" allows for a careful analysis of systems that produce oppression and mechanisms of resistance. In the chapters that follow, I trace how digital Black feminists work in the cracks of the matrix, exposing its fault lines. Adding digital to Black feminist thought reaffirms the matrix's existence and provides new possibilities for resistance.

## Hip-Hop Feminism and Shades of Gray

The Black women intellectuals and activists that Collins writes about and the race women that Brittney Cooper documents in her book *Beyond Respectability* lay much of the foundation for how I have discussed the origins of Black feminism thus far. In her foundational text *Black Feminist Thought*, Collins explains that Black women who are not often considered intellectuals have crafted Black feminism. Writing about the disconnect between feminism and her own experience, author and journalist Joan Morgan (2000) explains, "The sistas in my immediate proximity grew up in the 'hood, summered in the Hamptons, swapped spit on brightly lit Harlem corners, and gave up more than a li'l booty in Ivy League dorms. They were ghetto princesses with a predilection for ex-drug dealers. They got their caesars cut at the barbershop and perms at the Dominican's uptown. They were mack divas who rolled with posses fifteen bitches deep, and lived for Kappa beach parties, the Garage, the Roxy, and all things Hip-Hop" (p. 37–38). Both deeply poetic and profound, Morgan's words speak to the contradiction between the Black feminist figures she studied in college and the Black women of her everyday life. The gulf between them was not their politics but their experiences. The Black women with whom she most related looked, danced, drank, and lived as she did. Black feminist foremothers, she assumed, did not. Morgan's "crew" was not disconnected from the politics of Black feminism; instead, their lives were perhaps too big and unwieldy for Black feminism as she understood it to explain. Her college-educated crew never disengaged from their block, their culture, or their love of hip-hop. But their love of hip-hop did not align with those who saw the music and culture as antithetical to a path to Black women's liberation. This perceived disconnect prevented a full-throated embrace of feminism for many Black women in the 1990s. Because she and many other Black women of a certain age viewed Black feminism as unable to grapple with the contradictions of their lived experiences and the theories they read in books, Black feminism felt incomplete. What she argued for instead was a form of Black feminism comfortable with contradictions.

Morgan (2000) coined the term *hip-hop feminist* to describe a generation of Black feminists that live within the seemingly contradictory space of abhorring patriarchy while embracing the culture of hip-hop. Feminist scholars have criticized hip-hop for sexist lyrics, misogynistic representations of women, and its celebration of consumer capitalist culture. As Morgan explains, "The manifestos of Black feminism, while they helped me to understand the importance of articulating language to combat oppression, didn't give me the language to explore things that were not Black and white, but things that were in the gray.... And that gray is very much represented in Hip-Hop" (Ofori-Atta, 2011, para. 10). Hip-hop feminism, as articulated by the experience of Morgan, specifically focused on a generation of women who felt maligned by a perceived rigidity within Black feminist thought. For this group of Generation X and older millennials, hip-hop was not just a preferred musical genre; it was foundational to their experiences as Black women. Hip-hop informed their sense of self, belonging, and community. As Durham, Cooper, and Morris explain, "The creative, intellectual work of Hip-Hop feminism invites new questions about embodied experience, and offers alternative models for critical engagement" (Durham et al., 2013, p. 722). Rather than a world of black and white, it invites and welcomes the gray.

When bell hooks writes that Beyoncé is a terrorist and wonders aloud about the impact that Beyoncé has on young girls (hooks, 2016), she does so to provoke a challenge to a feminism that is not anti-imperialist and anticapitalist.[9] The responses that followed from hip-hop feminists illuminated the gulf between hooks's reading of Beyoncé and the comfort hip-hop feminism finds with "the gray." Brittney Cooper responded to hooks, saying, "She trots out the 'what about the children argument' as a way to police how Beyoncé styles and presents her body. Black women should be able to be publicly grown and sexy without suffering the accusation that our sexuality is harmful, especially to children" (King, 2014). After the release of *Lemonade* in 2016, Jamilah Lemieux wrote this of hooks's critique of the album and singer: "How detached from the hearts and minds of Black women does someone have to be to distill 'Lemonade' down to 'the business of capitalist money making at its best'? If all commercial art is commodity, does that really mean that creating a work that centers Black women in a beautiful way and speaks directly to and about us is rendered valueless because it's available to be consumed by all? And what does this say about the dozens of books she's published, presumably none of them available for free? Her speaking engagements?" (Lemieux, 2016, para. 7).[10] Janet Mock took to her Facebook page to press hooks on her "dismissal of Black femmes," arguing, "Femme feminists/writers/thinkers/artists are consistently dismissed, pressured to transcend presentation in order to prove our woke-ability" (Mock, 2016). To hip-hop feminists, Beyoncé is a public manifestation of the contradictions with which they have wrestled and made peace. Cooper, Lemieux, and Mock demonstrate the comfort that hip-hop feminists have found in shades of gray that hip-hop feminism embraces. As Tanisha Ford, professor at UMass-Amherst, explains, the stark differences in their readings demonstrate that "Black women of different generations, of different social classes, of different life experiences, will read and interpret Beyoncé differently" (King, 2014, para. 5). Hip-hop feminism is not unconcerned with critiques of capitalism or the male gaze. Instead, it relies on a long-standing history of Black women forced to reconcile their community, culture, and politics. From this vantage point, they challenge hooks's judgment, which finds Beyoncé's feminism lacking. Can you love *Lemonade* and be a feminist? Can you recognize the contradictions of Black female agency and the male gaze bound together in femme presentation? Morgan explains that she needs a feminism that allows her to grapple with "decidedly un-PC" questions. As she explains, "I need a feminism brave enough to fuck with the grays" (Morgan, 2000, p. 59). Hip-hop feminists seek a more complex, "functional feminism." Often writing from outside the academy, hip-hop feminists theorize new possibilities for Black feminism. Crunk Feminist Collective (CFC), which constitutes a group of hip-hop feminist activists, writers, and scholars, argues for percussive feminism. As CFC explains, "The tension between competing and often contradictory political and cultural projects like Hip-Hop and feminism is percussive in that it is both disruptive and generative" (Durham et al.,

2013, p. 724). Their feminism, like their hip-hop, is layered, sampled, and filled with the juxtaposition of many voices. Hip-hop as a genre, a cultural production, and a way of life informs how these women came to Black feminist thought and how they have reconstructed it in new ways.

In the long history of Black feminist thought, Black women have had ample practice living in spaces that asked them to be breadwinners and homemakers, strong and independent, while passive and submissive. But hip-hop requires a generation of Black feminists to publicly welcome the unwieldy gray areas of what happens when theory meets praxis. Morgan's articulation of hip-hop feminism gives us a point at which to observe a turn in Black feminist thought marked by Black women's relationship with the art, product, and lifestyle of hip-hop and their public insistence that we embrace the "gray." In *She Begat This*, Morgan (2018) reflects on the twentieth anniversary of Lauryn Hill's 1998 album *Miseducation of Lauryn Hill*. In the first chapter, Morgan describes a conversation with her goddaughter about the twentieth anniversary. Her goddaughter, now in her thirties, was a young teen at the time of the release and now views the singer/rapper as "judgy," with her lyrics often signaling respectability and "Hotep tendencies."[11] Morgan is defensive of the album, which was and remains so essential to hip-hop and hip-hop feminism. She explains that her goddaughter's view of hip-hop is shaped by the fact that she did not grow up in it. Hip-hop feminists view Hill as a vanguard—her work broke boundaries and provided an image of a Black woman successful in hip-hop on her own terms. A hip-hop feminist's view of Hill as a lyricist wrestling with issues of class and sexuality in 1998 is different from her goddaughter, who was birthed into hip-hop's ubiquity in American culture. Hip-hop permeated the style of dress, romantic relationships, media representations, and hip-hop feminists' intellectual pursuits. However, there is now a generation of Black feminists for whom Hill carries a different meaning. Black feminists who came of age in the early 2000s had their middle and high school years soundtracked by conscious rappers and neo soul artists, but corporatized hip-hop took over in their adulthood. They recognize misogyny and homophobia as features of the "urban" music made for white audiences. For these feminists, Hill is no revolutionary, and hip-hop is not the cultural moment that informs their brand of feminism. Instead, the digital turn informs how this group of Black feminists write, listen, produce, commune, and shape the principles of Black feminist thought for a new generation.

So hip-hop feminism provides us a model for marking another critical turn in the legacy of Black feminist thought. The importance of digital communication and technology in the lives of Black feminists today cannot be overstated. As a site of thought generation, community formation, and economic advancement, digital tools and culture have changed how Black women (and all people) interact with the world. As the second component of Black feminist technoculture, hip-hop feminism provides a road map for the messy work of unsettling assumptions about Black feminist principles, praxes, and products.

## From Technophobia to Black Technophilia

Many studying Black technoculture spent their early careers working against a prevailing belief that the new digital world left Black folks behind. Digital divide rhetoric, used to request more support and funding for "underserved" populations, implied an absence of Black folks in tech. Survey data suggested that Black households did not have access to broadband or desktop computing and, therefore, were missing a fundamental cultural shift in the late 1990s and early 2000s (Prieger & Hu, 2008). We were told Black America's future would be grim without training on and sustained access to technology. In 2009, Anna Everett described the dominant mode of understanding Black interaction with technology as Black technophobia. The myth of Black technophobia emerged from the mainstream press's "condescension, ghettoization, trivialization, and a general dismissiveness" about Black technology use (Everett, 2009, pp. 133–34). Through the digital divide lens, reporters and researchers considered Black Americans less than ideal users in the early cyber age. It seemed that the press thought it laughable that a group of people so inept and backward in their technology use could have much understanding or utility of digital technology. In addition to news reporting, internet studies also failed to capture Black users online. But a 2010 Pew report (A. Smith, 2010) affirmed Black users overindexing in their use of mobile phones to access the web. With a reputable agency like Pew providing cover, those of us who insisted that Black users were (1) real and (2) not deficient in their use of technology found a new voice. As Charlton McIlwain points out in *Black Software*, "The people who have widely used and mastered the digital tools that fueled Black Lives Matter and today's broader racial justice movement reflect and required a prior technical and political socialization" (McIlwain, 2019, p. 6).

In part, the failure to understand Black internet use was due to stereotypes about Black Americans that consciously and subconsciously pervade intellectual thought in America. The downplaying of Black ingenuity and creativity created a chasm between actual use and perceived use. Also, those writing about technology were not connected to Black culture. Instead, scholars offered euphoric predictions of the internet, suggested technology as the savior of the marginalized, and positioned digital tools as a beacon of anticapitalistic and antihegemonic light. These uncritical utopic views came from a sense of optimism about technology's capabilities to change human interaction and expand the possibilities of democracy to all (Papacharissi, 2002). However, metaphors of a new frontier or "new world" hearken back to the West's nostalgia for the Americas' imperial conquest (Papacharissi, 2010). The optimism of this "digital frontier" demonstrates our collective refusal to deal with how technology reinforces systems of power and an absence of critical race scholarship in much of early internet studies.

Everett's (2009) work contradicts a myth of Black technophobia by introducing the reality of Black technophilia. Steering away from simplistic and uncritical metaphors, Everett argues that the internet provides a context where African diasporic traditions are not bound by a nation-state or "volatile press-government relationships," fostering the pursuit of "emancipation and liberation" (Everett, 2009, pp. 35–48). Laying out the rich technological and Afro-futurist tradition of Africans living in the diaspora, Everett cites the work of Mark Dery, Greg Tate, Tricia Rose, and Samuel Delany. She uses the Million Woman March in October 1997 as a case to document Black women's strategic use of the "internet's counter logic of decentralization to reposition themselves at the center of public life in America, if only for a day" (Everett, 2009, p. 78). The march drew a crowd of approximately five hundred thousand, with organizers advocating for sisterhood, economic development, and unity among Black women. While the Million Woman March did not garner the same national attention as the Million Man March, the exhibition of Black women's communicative and technological expertise is a reason to still take note of the event. Without sponsorship from national organizations, Black women maximized their knowledge of online media and technological systems. Organizers used word of mouth, Black-owned media, and the internet to raise awareness about the event. Black technophilia was on full display.

This concept that Everett calls "Black technophilia" explains the unique relationship Black Americans have with technology. Marisa Parham (2018) describes Black culture as "digital before digital caught up." Adam Banks (2010) positions DJs as griots, using analogies of turntables, breaks, and remix culture to chart Black oral traditions from the analog to the digital. Banks maps features like mixing, remixing, and sampling as elements that predate the digital. Rayvon Fouché explains that "Black technological activities cannot be effectively categorized within the dominant canon of science and technology" and redirects our gaze to what he calls "Black vernacular technological creativity" (Fouché, 2006, p. 642). He explains Black vernacular technological creativity results "from resistance to existing technology and strategic appropriations of the material and symbolic power and energy of technology." Black vernacular technological creativity engages in practices of redeployment, reconception, and recreation to "enable African American people to reclaim different levels of technological agency" (p. 641). André Brock (2020) has referred to a "natural affinity" that Black users have for the internet. Using libidinal economy, critical race theory, and science and technology studies, Brock explains that Black folks have become digital ingénues and technophiles. His work contradicts Black technophobia but also critiques Afro-futurism as the way to understand Black technological prowess. Instead, Brock argues that Afro-futurism misses the "banality and everydayness" of Black Twitter or other spaces where "ratchet digital practice" is enacted. He situates Black technocultural studies in the "post present" and insists we "reinvest futurity into present uses of the digital, rather than in possible Black cyborg or Black magical futures" (Brock, 2020, pp. 218–19). Each scholar cited above wrestles against the myth of Black technophobia, pointing to the past, present, or future of Blackness as intertwined with technology.

Black technophilia is the third analytical component of the virtual beauty shop. Technophilia rejects Black technological deficiency and allows for a long historical look at Black folks' relationship with technology. Technophilia reminds us that Black people do not need saving when it comes to aptitude and access to technology. Instead, Black technophilia holds the possibility of seeing the expanse of digital capacities while acknowledging the continuing ways that the digital reifies systems of power and control in our society. I chart Black feminist technoculture as simultaneously congruent with the past, marked by the immediacy of the present, and with hope toward a digital Black feminist future.

## The Virtual Beauty Shop and Black Feminist Technoculture

The virtual beauty shop provides a theoretical and practical approach to studying Black feminist discourse in the digital age. Together, the matrix of domination, hip-hop feminism's shades of gray, and Black technophilia provide the critical lens to understand the relationships between Black feminism and technology. The beauty shop gives way to a robust analysis of Black feminist technoculture that stretches across decades and tools. The technology of Black hair care professionals within the beauty shop and the relationships they form with their clients preview the technological prowess of Black bloggers and online writers in navigating new technologies of communication. Digital technology, like all technologies before, interpolates with its users. It is not possible to study digital technologies without considering the history and culture of those using them. The beauty shop's history shows Black women's technical capabilities, agency, and creation of worlds of opportunity for themselves. However, the shop also serves as a useful metaphor because of its complicated relationships with capitalism, colorism, and patriarchy. For all the brilliance and technical expertise housed within the shop, Black hair care and Black beauty shop owners are not exempt from white supremacist and patriarchal norms and social class inequity.

Black feminist discourse is now constructed, disseminated, challenged, and consumed using digital technology. This intervention has a profound impact on the discourse itself. In the following three chapters, I engage with the principles and praxes of digital Black feminism and interrogate digital Black feminism as a product. I consider Black feminist use of digital technology and the impact that this has on digital Black feminists' ability to continue the Black feminist tradition of dismantling racial and gendered oppression and breaking free of imperialism and capitalism. Black women's lives are wrought with interlocking systems of oppression. However, digital Black feminism is transformative in combatting hegemonic rule because of these interlocking systems. I begin the following chapter by tracing the evolution of Black feminist principles in the blogosphere.

3

# Principles for a Digital Black Feminism, or Blogging While Black

In March of 2020, *Hair Love* won the Academy Award for Best Animated Short Film. Produced by Matthew Cherry, the animated film tells the story of a little girl whose mother is a natural hair vlogger.[1] While the mom is hospitalized with cancer, the girl's father uses her vlog to learn to do his daughter's hair. Cherry created a Kickstarter campaign to crowdsource funding for the project, raising over $300,000. He posted short animations on social media and created a buzz for the project, with celebrities like Gabrielle Union and Yara Shahidi signing on as coproducers. *Hair Love* creates a dynamic representation of the relationship between a Black father, his daughter, and her hair. But it also subtly reminds us of how vital digital communication is in circulating and producing affirming content for Black content creators. Both Cherry and the mother in the film rely on digital media in their role as producers. In the film, the mother's work as a vlogger makes it possible for the father to attend to his daughter's hair. Because many who look to these sites for help may be new to their natural hair journey, blogger and vlogger guidance are critical to maintaining the health of their hair. Natural hair vlogs and blogs continue to serve an essential need in the Black community, offering practical guidance on hair maintenance and a community of support. While other social media sites have since become more popular, bloggers in the previous decades created and maintained spaces for Black folks to learn, to dialogue, and to build community.

Blogging was popularized in the early 2000s when the addition of free platforms like Blogger meant more users could create and publish content without needing coding skills.[2] Communication and internet researchers rightly turned their attention to the value blogs brought to political discourse and consumer culture. In his book *Blogs, Wikipedia,*

*Second Life, and Beyond: From Production to Produsage*, media scholar Axel Bruns (2008) outlines how bloggers shifted from users to creators and changed how we understand concepts like production and consumption in a digital age. Blogs offered internet users a new power to manage content, index news and information, and form a community of like-minded readers with similar interests or experiences. Blogs also offered a way to monetize writing and other skills online. Black women bloggers transformed the blogosphere into a virtual beauty shop wherein they could make a living, service other Black women, and demonstrate their understanding of the power of branding.

Blogging provides a unique space for the creation and maintenance of alternate rhetorical spheres for Black Americans. Research on Black Twitter has highlighted the platform for short retorts and hashtags as means of utilizing communicative devices like signifyin' and playing the dozens (Brock, 2012; Florini, 2013).[3] Black Twitter has been the most popular site for social media inquiry in recent years. The work of internet scholars like André Brock, Sarah Florini, and Meredith Clark in the last decade has been groundbreaking in many ways, causing internet researchers to consider signifying practices, resistance, activism, and ratchet digital practice online. The increased attention on Black Twitter has allowed researchers to engage in a more nuanced discussion about Black technoculture. However, the overfocus on Twitter reflects some researcher's bias toward the platform. Twitter is one of the more accessible apps to mine for data. Because it is primarily a text-based app and because Twitter's API is available, researchers can use hashtags and key terms to pull countless tweets.[4] Computational software can run sentiment analysis and network analysis and do coding on a data set of a million or more tweets. Researchers and journalists may also focus on the app because they use it more frequently than other sites and apps to network, engage in self-promotion, and distribute their work. Recently, cross-platform analysis has gotten some traction, as has research into other platforms like Instagram and TikTok. However, all social media apps can trace their origins to the blogosphere. As Jill Walker Rettberg explains, "Blogs were social media years before the term was coined and, in many ways, blogs still form the backbone of social media. Far more people are on Facebook or another social media platform than there are bloggers, but much of what we do in social media is at root a form of blogging" (Rettberg, 2014, p. 14). Because most research on blogging happened in the early 2000s before the *discovery* of Black Twitter and Pew's 2010 report on Black users' overindexing of social media, internet inquiry missed a lot of the rich history of the Black blogosphere.

In this chapter, I consider the impact of digital communication on Black feminist thought by examining the principles created and adopted in a Black feminist blogosphere. In the blogosphere, Black feminist thinkers, through long-form writing, community building, and digital archiving, began to craft foundational principles for digital Black feminist rhetoric that we now see on sites like Twitter and Instagram. Blogging provided a landscape for digital Black feminists to work out principles through dialogue protected from outside interference within the virtual beauty shop. Black feminist enclaves like the natural hair vlog in *Hair Love* hide counterhegemonic ideas for protection and survival. Unlike Twitter, wherein groups may seek to engage with other publics to foster protests or boycotts, bloggers formed an alternate public to refashion Black feminism in the digital age outside the gaze of the dominant group. While posting recommendations for hair care products, discussing Beyoncé, or watching *Scandal* each week, Black feminist bloggers advocated for emancipatory freedom and reconceptualized liberation within a digital framework. They navigated the matrix of domination and found strategies to engage in critical resistance using digital tools. The principles formed by Black feminist thinkers in the blogosphere are not only articulated online but *exist* because of Black feminist's relationship to digital culture. From 2014 to 2020, I regularly engaged with the blogs cited in this chapter. During that time, I read news posts and participated in the blogging communities through commenting. I analyzed both the content of posts and comments and the sites themselves for insight into how Black feminists craft new principles and the digital environments in which they form. From this study, I chart five principles bloggers used to make rhetorical arguments for Black feminism. They prioritize agency, reclaim the right to self-identify, centralize gender nonbinary spaces of discourse, create complicated allegiances, and insert a dialectic of self and community interests. In the pages that follow,

I explain these principles and how their development is made possible through bloggers' interactions with digital technology.

## Agency

Readers of the blog *A Belle in Brooklyn* were greeted in March of 2014 by the pop-up, fifteen-second advertisement for OraQuick, an HIV home testing kit. Demetria Lucas, the sole contributing writer and founder of *A Belle in Brooklyn*, was a paid endorser for the product. The blog featured a banner ad for the test kit, which was the only product featured on this blog aside from Lucas's (2014a) book *Don't Waste Your Pretty*. The blog's tagline was "The Perspective of a Southern Woman Living above the Mason Dixon." The site's background was dark pink/purple, and next to the blog's title was an icon created by combing three hearts on their side that graduate in color from pink to black. Scrolling down the opening page, readers encountered posts in reverse chronological order buttressed with advertisements on the screen's right side. Lucas invited users to share her posts on social media and subscribe to her newsletter. In the about section of the site, Lucas described herself as a former and current journalist, life/relationship coach, and star of a reality show on the Bravo television network. Lucas listed her educational background in this section as well. It is clear from the emphasis on her persona how central she was to forming the content and shaping the conversations on the site.

*A Belle in Brooklyn* was self-promoting but not self-aggrandizing. As the blog was one arm of Lucas's bourgeoning relationship-advice business, her posts fell into two main categories: advice-response posts to readers' questions and personal diary-like entries that used Lucas's own life to provide guidance. The blog was not about celebrity culture, so when Lucas mentioned a celebrity, the focus was on their business, friendships, or intimate relationships as a catalyst to discuss broader relationship issues. Lucas's guidance was a mixture of progressive feminist appeals and traditional southern sensibilities—this seemingly contradictory position harkening to Morgan's "shades of gray." Around the time of bell hooks's initial public critique of Beyoncé, Lucas wrote about the singer's self-titled album as it related to her conception of feminism.

On December 17, 2014, Demetria Lucas published "6 Things I Care About on 'Beyoncé' More Than Her Feminism" on her blog and for the *Root*.[5] In the post, Lucas mocks public debate about Beyoncé's feminism, insisting one cannot determine if Beyoncé is a feminist based solely on an album release. Instead, Lucas asked us to focus on six things that are more interesting and important about the album:

1. Release of the album without press or advertising;
2. A lyric from the song "Drunk in Love" that appears to reference Ike and Tina Turner's tumultuous relationship;
3. A song called "Rocket" that exudes sexuality from a female perspective;
4. A reference to her miscarriage in the song "Heaven";
5. Introducing the world to the term Surfbording (a sex position);
6. And her new persona that raps and breaks with the good girl image she formed over a decade in the industry. (Lucas, 2014b)

Lucas's list points to the agency of Beyoncé as a woman, an artist, and a businessperson. She uses the second item as an opportunity to advocate for both creative control and sexual agency for Beyoncé. The line "Eat the cake, Anna Mae" from the song "Drunk in Love" comes from the film *What's Love Got to Do with It*.[6] In the song, Beyoncé and her husband use "cake" to reappropriate the negative connotation from the film and reframe it within a song about sex with a consenting partner. The line connects Black listeners to a cultural touchstone, and as Lucas argues, it does not suggest that Beyoncé condones domestic violence. Lucas castigates the knee-jerk reaction of many critics for taking the idea out of context. Lucas's reading of the line and song suggests that one can abhor domestic violence while understanding reference to an abuser does not necessarily condone abuse. This nuanced approach to discussing patriarchy is a feature of digital Black feminism that builds upon its predecessor, hip-hop feminism. Hip-hop feminists granted Black women permission to love the Black men and music many deemed problematic. In the previous chapter, I outlined the pushback hooks received from many hip-hop feminists who found freedom in Joan Morgan's "shades of gray." Digital Black feminists not only "fuck with the grays" but champion the grays as the primary principle of their feminism. Digital Black feminism openly challenges critics of Black culture who speak without consideration for context, intent, and implications.

Lucas's list highlights individual agency and an unwillingness to have others define/label what is problematic and patriarchal or what could be considered feminist and progressive. For digital Black feminists like Lucas, Beyoncé Knowles-Carter's song lyrics redeploy "problematic" imagery for her purposes and sexual agency. Beyoncé (as a character in the song and video) is sexually aroused by this man and by his words. Lucas explains that Beyoncé not only speaks about her sexuality but locates her sexual pleasure as the most crucial component of her sexual encounters. She is sexual but not sexualized. Her agency creates possibilities for the former and challenges the latter. People can sexualize the image of Beyoncé, but for digital Black feminists, Knowles-Carter's agency supersedes this concern.

While the second item on Lucas's list focuses on sexual agency, bloggers in the early days of digital Black feminism are just as concerned about their political and financial agency. They argue that the ability to succeed financially as a Black woman is personally beneficial but can also damage patriarchal white supremacy. Lucas defends Beyoncé's financial and economic agency as an artist. Since she issues this defense in an online blogging community that supports her livelihood, Lucas's defense of Beyoncé is also a defense of herself as an entrepreneur and someone who produces feminist content. Lucas's status as an entrepreneur whose blogging contributes to her financial well-being does not negate that her work on the blog is valuable to a community of Black women readers. Agency itself lives in the messy gray area between being a key feature of Black feminist blogging principle and a feature of neoliberal individualism. Lucas devotes lucrative revenue-generating advertising space to only two concerns, the promotion of her book and a company providing at-home HIV tests. She does not separate her business decisions from her ability to use *A Belle in Brooklyn* to promote ideals of sexual health and reverse the stigma around HIV in the Black community. *A Belle in Brooklyn* is a virtual beauty shop that functions as a tool of self-promotion while providing generative and affirming content to Black women. While mainstream blogs and news sites were also captivated by Beyoncé's album, Lucas's virtual beauty shop controls the dialogue and refines digital Black feminist principles. Bloggers own their "shops" and therefore set the parameters for participation in dialogue within this space. Digital Black feminists use the virtual beauty shop to work out the intricacies of how this form of Black feminism will deal with issues like sexual and financial agency.

Digital Black feminism proposes that individual agency for Black women is necessary to achieve liberation from white supremacy and patriarchy. As Maria del Guadalupe Davidson makes clear, agency has a long history in Black feminist thought. She explains, "To act like an agent and to be perceived as an agent—is a call to be more than a thing and to gain the power of resistance to the agency of others" (Davidson, 2019, p. 19). Davidson argues that there is a gap between traditional Black feminism and millennial feminism based on their different treatments of agency. Popular music and sex work are two spaces where scholars identify a generational chasm between traditional Black feminists and "millennial feminists." The former sees the oversexualization of Black women's bodies; the latter suggests that Black women are sexual beings and agents in full control of using their bodies sexually (Davidson, 2019). bell hooks's primary critique of Beyoncé is functionally a critique of agency as an organizing principle of Black feminism thought. For traditional Black feminist scholars, agency is bound to systems like capitalism. Discussing "lifestyle feminism," bell hooks argues if your feminism "colludes with systems that harm women" (Dionne, 2017) or if you could "fit feminism into [your] existing lifestyle" (hooks, 2000b), then it is no longer a tool used to disrupt oppression. But rather than fitting feminism into their lifestyle or merely conforming to a capitalistic idealization of individual agency, digital Black feminists are reforming Black feminism's relationship to the concept of agency. The difference in how Black feminists conceptualize agency is a product of their relationship with digital technology.

As taken up by digital Black feminists, agency signals Black women's ability to master and adopt a strategy for liberation that intentionally pulls at the most salient features of neoliberal American culture, personal liberty and individualism. Just as race women of the early 1900s used respectability as a rhetorical strategy, online writers in the digital era of Black feminism use the language and beliefs of their white dominant class to strip the logic of their exclusion (B. C. Cooper, 2017; Higginbotham, 1993; Wolcott, 2001). When U.S. culture and laws excluded

Black women from womanhood, respectability provided a path for entry and a tool to undo racist logic. In this century, embracing agency works against the racist logic that supports Black women's exclusion from the mythology and history of digital technology. For digital Black feminists, agency redefines the self as powerful and skillful within systems of technology and digital culture. Rather than being trapped by the gaze, controlling images, or oversexualizing the Black female body, digital Black feminists suggest that controlling their bodies and images *online* is transformative and transgressive, no matter who is watching. Through their entanglement with digital technology, they develop platforms to reconceive the very concept of agency. The digital affords—even demands—that users become producers. Blogging and other early digital communities require individuals to produce a profitable space for dialogue and exchange, just as Lucas and many other entrepreneurial bloggers did. While seemingly provoked by opposite beliefs about women and freedom, both respectability in the early 1900s and agency in the 2000s are strategies used by Black feminists to achieve their goals. Both strategies traffic in ideologies upheld by capitalism and deployed within racial projects of liberalism (Omi & Winant, 1998). Yet we should not conclude from their deployment that either group of Black feminist thinkers is unaware of how white folks cause harm with respectability or agency. Instead, we can read the use of these tropes of Americana as an intentional strategy of dismantling white supremacy. Thus far, it is unclear that such a strategy can be successful over the long term. Does the tacit acceptance of capitalism and neoliberalism or the use of a Talented Tenth philosophy, even strategically, destroy this generation's claims to a Black feminist politic? While in the preface to the list Lucas asserts that she is not interested in a debate about Beyoncé as a feminist, the body of her post articulates a feminist ideology that is reflective of the newly forming digital Black feminism. So is Beyoncé a feminist? According to digital Black feminists, it is not anyone's concern or within anyone but the individual's power to determine whether she is a feminist. Agency, as evoked by digital Black feminists, unsettles the idea that anyone can determine who you are better than you can.

## The Right to Self-Identify

The Black blogosphere is not a monolith. While blogs like *A Belle in Brooklyn* crafted principles within a virtual beauty shop, other bloggers utilized different strategies to provoke debate among readers. In May of 2014, the writer of *The Field Negro* described himself as "raised in the house, but field certified." Wayne Bennett, the founder of *The Field Negro*, was featured in the *Root*, *Black Enterprise*, and a variety of other news sources. In stark contrast to Demetria Lucas, who uses her persona to connect with readers and establish her brand, Bennett does not identify himself by name on the site, instead referring to himself only as "Field" or "Mr. Field" on posts. *Field Negro* privileges an authoritative and journalistic style rather than a diary-like or community structure.

Positioning himself as an objective arbiter of facts, Bennett's rhetorical strategy on the site mirrors many mainstream political blogs of this era. Bennett's posts provoke debate among readers, unsettling readers' perspectives and pushing them toward political action. Commenters do not need to create an account to post, nor must they label their post with any name to respond to Bennet's provocations. They may reply directly to one another and often do so with profanity, hate speech, and racially offensive language. Commenters frequently monopolize threads with personal battles and insults directed often between only two or three parties. Because this is a Blogspot blog, Bennett could set controls to approve comments and delete those he deems unacceptable. However, the author chooses to leave the comments open, pushing for a transparent debate among opposing parties. Commenters, therefore, have no means to report abusive posts. The debates on sites like *Field Negro* do not require the familiarity or conviviality necessary for a sustained community.

In this era, Black feminist bloggers relied heavily on named participation among readers by using avatars, screen names, and "about" pages to create familiarity among readers. When the Black blogosphere began to explode, Black feminist bloggers took cues from popular social networking sites in establishing new norms on their platforms. Transferring their social networking skills from sites like BlackPlanet,[7] Myspace, or Facebook required participants to create a profile, including a name and personal information. Users were required to identify themselves to participate in public debate online in these spaces. Social networking sites and blogs provide users with repeated practice using screen names, images, and profiles to identify themselves to other users. Logging in, creating an avatar, and selecting and changing a handle or username is a normative part of social interaction for those who came of age with social networking services. When geographic proximity is lacking, on-line communities share values, practices, or beliefs to build community. Offline community groups based on belonging to a racial, ethnic, or gender group require visual confirmation of likeness for participation. Online, signifiers like race and gender may not be immediately appar-ent unless an individual chooses to reveal them through their use of language or their avatar or profile. Beyond a possible affordance of the platform, this feature is a driving force behind the right to self-identify as a principal feature of Black feminist discourse online.

In the Black feminist blogosphere, bloggers craft the "about" sections on blogs by providing a detailed explanation of themselves, their moti-vation for writing, and their identities. When Black feminist bloggers create an online brand for their site, users are motivated to do the same as they participate in the community discourse. In the virtual beauty shop, bloggers and community members created avatar versions of themselves who would interact online—versions of self they were will-ing to present to the world. In so doing, participants made decisions about both self-presentation and identity. Replicating this in blogs, mul-tiple social media sites, and gaming platforms meant that digital Black feminist thinkers have long had to consider the public performance of self online. Everyone coming of age in the digital era has practiced this online performance of self. But Black women considered deviant and "other" in American society had extra practice in navigating their sense of self in stark contrast to societal expectations. Collins (Collins, 2009) explains that mediated images of Black women are often a tool of he-gemonic control within the matrix of domination. Likewise, Kishonna Gray describes how Black video gamers face racist provocations as play-ers navigate gaming communities while possessing "deviant" identities (Gray, 2012). The vitriol faced by Black "deviant" gamers occurs because others form perceptions of them offline and bring those perceptions to their online interactions. Digital Black feminists encountered the ideo-logical weaponry described by Gray and Collins before they ever began blogging. Their self-identification is a political decision, intentionally resistant to the kind of othering that hegemonic whiteness practices daily. Because of the vitriol for their offline identities, digital Black feminist blogging establishes the principle of the right to self-identify, asserting that they alone have the power to name themselves as feminists, as Black, and as women.

Digital Black feminists recognize the power and political implications of self-naming and claim it as a right that has previously been withheld from them. Blogging on the site *For Harriet*, Shannon Luders-Manuel describes herself as a Black woman with a white parent and explains how important this identification became in a post–Trayvon Martin and post-Ferguson era. In an August 12, 2015, post titled "What It Means to Be Mixed Race during the Fight for Black Lives," Luders-Manuel explains that she has always viewed herself as Black (Luders-Manuel, 2015). However, identifying with Blackness at a time when her white family or colleagues would prefer a more palatable biracial version of her is intentional. Her self-identification does not darken her skin or assign her more Afrocentric features, but it is rhetorically and politically resistant to a system of white supremacy. The one-drop rule gave people of mixed-race parentage no agency in their racial classification, designating them as Black regardless of their phenotype. However, in an Obama age of postraciality,[8] those of mixed heritage were dubbed "reverse racists"[9] for failing to acknowledge they are also white. The politics of mixed-race identity is complex yet has always acted in furtherance of white supremacist goals. Whether those of mixed-race served as an argument for antimiscegenation laws or "proof" of the country's move to postraciality, the right to self-identify did not belong to this group. Luders-Manuel forcefully reasserts the right to self-identify, which is a principle born of the medium of blogging.

Within the virtual beauty shop of a blog like *For Harriet*, Black feminist writers can explore the extensions and limitations of self-identification as a principle of digital Black feminism. *For Harriet* is a blogging community constructed by Black feminists to foster enclaved discourse. Its founder, Kimberly Nicole Foster, describes the site as "a blog community for women of African Ancestry" (www.forharriet .com). Bloggers on the site, like Luders-Manuel, all provide a bio at the end of their posts. Commenting on the site requires a log-in and a name using Twitter, Facebook, Google, or Disqus. Leaving a comment leaves a means of identifying oneself. The posts do not provoke, nor is there evidence of outside groups or contentious debates in the comments. The lively discussion on the site is an in-group activity within the shop that focuses on the community's needs rather than attempting to prove importance or worth to outsiders. Discussions can be complicated and contentious, yet the site's affordances, including the requirement that participants be named, ensure that they are comfortable with comments attributed to their name and image. Luders-Manuel wades through challenging waters to make claims on her right to self-identify and, in so doing, requires readers to test whether self-identification as a principle serves the aims of liberation or constraint for digital Black feminists.

## Gender Nonbinary Spaces of Discourse

Serena Williams is arguably the most dominant athlete of our time. Serena Williams is also a woman whose brown skin, athleticism, and curvaceous frame often spark the ire of those who believe a dainty, white form marks womanhood. From the early stages of their careers, the Williams' sisters have dominated the tennis world. Simultaneously, the pair's media coverage has been dominated by body-shaming, racist criticism, and outright lies about their bodies and skills. Fellow athletes have joked that playing against Serena Williams is like "playing a man" (Christopher, 2009, chap. 6, sec. 2, para. 12). Critics have all but accused her of doping to change her body and improve her game (Bryant, 2018). Williams has also faced critique from Black men comparing her body to that of a man. Embattled Black sports analyst Jason Whitlock described her body as an "unsightly layer of thick, muscled blubber" (Whitlock, 2009). As Black feminist bloggers began to write about Williams, they inserted into the dialogue more than a general critique of the racist and misogynistic tropes characterizing her coverage. Bloggers reminded us of the long legacy of Black women excluded from womanhood within a white supremacist society. Williams is a cis Black woman who faces criticism about her distance from white femininity. This critique and violence are only amplified when applied to Black trans women. Building on Black feminist foremothers' revolutionary work, bloggers did not seek inclusion into the sorority of white womanness. Instead, their work challenges the very binaries used to determine the boundaries of gender.

Trans women are killed in terrifyingly high numbers, and violence against trans women is staggering. Violence against Black trans women is even more alarming. According to the Human Rights Campaign, "In 2018, advocates tracked at least 26 deaths of transgender people in the U.S. due to fatal violence, the majority of whom were Black transgender women" (Human Rights Campaign, 2019). Forty percent of all hate violence crimes were targeted toward transgender women of color (Aspegren, n.d.).[10] Building upon their intimate knowledge of the matrix of domination, Black feminist bloggers must consider the implications of intimate partner violence coupled with transphobia that Black trans women face. On the blog *For Harriet*, Ashleigh Shackelford writes,

> In order to address our violence against Black transwomen, we have to be able to unpack gender expectations and the limitation of accessing femininity and/or womanhood. We cannot expect Black transwomen to have access to our ideas of femininity or "soft" womanhood when we've continued to fight for that same affirmed womanhood for centuries and have yet to achieve these standards we've been imprisoned to. Our humanity as Black ciswomen is more accessible because Black transwomen's distance from gender conformity is further than ours. That means our humanity is based upon the dehumanization of Black transwomen, hence our ability to enact our privilege and carry out this violence. Our ostensibly comfortable navigation of gender is based on the erasure of our Black trans sisters, and our silence and complacency in this reality is even more violent. (Shackelford, 2016, para. 7)

In attempts to solidify their place as "real" women in white society, some Black cis women have drawn firm lines of exclusion from their Black trans sisters. Yet as they become the "face" of trans violence, Black trans women force Black cis women to acknowledge their complicity in their matrix.

Monica Roberts tags her blog *Transgriot* as "a proud unapologetic Black trans woman speaking truth to power and discussing the world around her since 2006."[11] *Transgriot* features no advertising and has maintained the same layout for most of its existence. There is no menu bar or static content at the top or bottom of the page. The page has a white backdrop with posts of about five hundred words or more and images, and a continual reverse chronological feed dominates the center of the page. The left and right margins feature information about the site, disclaimers on using content from the site, and the Creative Commons license, along with archived content, links to other sites, and featured posts. Roberts is the only writer on the site, using her platform to discuss current news and entertainment and advocate for trans rights. The site's aesthetics, in 2019, are reminiscent of blogs of 2008 or 2009, making clear that the emphasis for this blogger is the content. Roberts's labor is twofold, maintaining the blog alone and the work of arguing her right to exist in each post. As Black trans folks like Roberts extend this offline labor online, they force Black feminism to reconcile with transphobia.

In 2014, Roberts wrote a series of posts dealing with racism within the trans community. When both Janet Mock[12] and Laverne Cox[13] received increased mainstream press and attention in 2014, *Transgriot* positioned the two as leaders of a modern movement built upon a long legacy of Black trans activism. In a post dated February 7, 2014, Roberts writes, "For the first time in the trans community's modern history, we have Black trans women like Janet Mock, Laverne Cox, my GLAAD Award-nominated self stepping up, getting the media spotlight and broadening the conversation. The appearances of Mock and Cox on the scene in the last two years and countless other African-American trans people have done more to advance the conversation and understanding about trans issues in the Black cis and SGL community and amongst our intelligentsia than those discussions on trans issues in the last six decades" (Roberts, 2014). Black trans and gender nonbinary folks doing radical feminist work is nothing new. Too often, though, cis-normative feminist revisionist history has ignored their work.

Some strains of feminism have essentialized experiences of womanhood to exclude those who are trans and ignore the experiences of those who are nonbinary. Vocal feminist advocate Chimamanda Ngozi Adichie gave an interview in 2017 suggesting that trans women had different experiences than cis women, implying that they were not real women (Newman, 2017). Though she later clarified her remarks, her initial comments remind us that Black women feminists are not immune from transphobic language. Some Black feminist leaders have critiqued the femme display of trans women as encouraging the male gaze and furthering patriarchal systems. At the New School in 2016, actress and trans activist Laverne Cox argued that occupying a nonnormative gender space was in itself transgressive (New School, 2014). Therefore, her femme gender display was also transgressive. Her assertions challenged Black feminists to consider that constructs like the male gaze were theorized by cis women and with cis women in mind. The assertion "ain't I a woman" carries more weight for Black trans women, whose womanness is questioned, ridiculed, and even used as an unjustifiable reason for violence against their bodies. Black cis women should recognize this, perhaps more than any other group. Digital Black feminists, both trans and cis, have openly critiqued any feminism that limits the expanses of womanness, recognizing that feminism that does not fiercely advocate for all women is no feminism at all.

Digital Black feminists, perhaps more than their feminist foremothers, have comfort outside of gender binaries. This comfort comes from socialization online, which trains them to see their work, identities, and lives outside of binaries. The digital requires a break in the common understanding of binaries like public and personal, work and play, virtual and real. Blogging and other online writing are profoundly personal, constructed for an enclaved community, yet available publicly to anyone who can locate the web address. Drafting ideas, threads, and memes on Twitter is part of the branding necessary to sustain employment but is also intentionally "libidinal, nonproductive, and inefficient" (Brock, 2020, p. 34). Online communities are often labeled virtual, yet people hold closer bonds than with their neighbors or coworkers with whom they have "real" relationships. Bloggers' embrace of online writing updates the narrow definitions of what constituted labor, play, community, publicity, and privacy. Coming to feminism when one must continuously sit comfortably outside of binary boxes makes this a moment where Black feminism is ready to contend with the reality of gender as both confining and liberating.

The Black feminist blogosphere created spaces for discourse outside of the binaries of gender. Both Black trans and cis bloggers have already pushed beyond the boundaries of societal expectations in their digital work. While the Black community, like the rest of society, must grapple with transphobia, digital Black feminists carve out principles that demand all Black folks have the right to exist as themselves. As Monica Roberts writes,

> So what is it about the simple demand of transpeople wanting to peacefully live our lives just like anyone else on the planet that scares the crap out of people? . . . Is it because it forces cis people who uncomfortable in their own skins to think about gender identity characteristics that people once thought were immutable? . . . Or is it because transpeople make cisfolks realize that the dividing line between masculine and feminine is not the rigid Berlin Wall binary many people envision it as but a thin line segment that we all fall along somewhere along? All we transpeople is [sic] around the world want is to proudly live our lives in our various nations just like any other cis person. (Roberts, 2013, paras. 5–6)

The principle of gender nonbinary acceptance and advocacy reflects a generational shift based on digital sensibilities. Black cis writers do not always get it right but fortunately still create allegiances with trans writers in the blogosphere. These allegiances shift Black feminist politics in the direction of being better equipped to fight for the freedom of all Black folks.

## Complicated Allegiances

On September 19, 2017, writer Damon Young of *Very Smart Brothas* penned the article "Straight Black Men Are the White People of Black People." Young describes how Black men are often complicit in the oppression and violence waged against Black women and are dedicated to misunderstanding their privilege (Young, 2017b). He does this by comparing the power that straight cis Black men hold within the Black community to the privilege white folks have in the larger society. He asks Black men to reflect upon their experiences with racism to unpack their male privilege and its impact on Black women and gender nonbinary folks. Unsurprisingly, Young was met with outrage from many Black men unwilling to concede his central premise, that "privilege exists on a spectrum." Some offered concern that his critique of male privilege within the Black community would activate negative stereotypes about Black men, a group already demonized in white society. As he explains, "As I read and watched and listened to some of those responses, I was flabbergasted at how similar what they were saying was to what white people say when accused of racism, and how blind they were to those similarities" (Young, 2018b, para. 6).

In 2009, Damon Young and Panama Jackson (writing under a pseudonym) started the blog *Very Smart Brothas* (*VSB*) without ever meeting in person; instead, they developed a digitally mediated writing relationship. Working with consultant and cofounder Liz Burr, *VSB* was originally imagined as a blog to tackle relationships, with Young and Jackson blogging about their dating lives. However, it quickly morphed into a humor and lifestyle blog where the pair talked about everything from hip-hop to the presidency. The two "very smart brothas" tackled issues related to their class status, racism in the workplace, their favorite television shows like *Scandal* and *Love & Hip Hop*, and later, their experiences as husbands and fathers.

Over the years, Jackson and Young carefully cultivated a community of dedicated readers. It was not uncommon in the early years of the blog for the bloggers to participate in long conversations via the comment section with readers. Readers commented with the expectation that the bloggers would respond, posing new questions and challenging the writers about their ideas. The community of participants, who selected usernames for participation, were so well known to each other that the responses sometimes deviated from the originally posted content. Commenters began side conversations about meetups, inquired about children and spouses, and even provided help to community members moving to new cities or parts of town. The group was tight-knit and recognized each other from their chosen screen names. Like Young and Jackson, most had never met in person in the early years yet considered themselves friends. *VSB* hosted the liveliest comments section of any of the sites I participated in or studied over the years. It was a community.

In 2017, *VSB* joined Gizmodo Media Group, whose parent company is Univision. Gizmodo, now G/O Media, also owns Jezebel,[14] the *Root*,[15] and the *Onion*.[16] *VSB* would become a vertical platform within the *Root*, providing Young and Jackson the opportunity for stability in their careers as writers and a new home for *VSB*. They could leave their nine-to-five jobs and focus exclusively on being editors and writers rather than managing the platform. Describing the move to their loyal readers, Young explains, "VSB will still be VSB (Young, 2017a)," but the move changed the community in significant ways. The move to the *Root* increased exposure to the blog. Cross-promotion and integration with other Gizmodo platforms meant that *VSB*'s posts, previously insulated within the enclave they created, would now be open to the flaming and trolling common on many A-list blogs. Young explores some of the mixed emotions of the integration in his classic sly humor, saying,

> We're giving up control of something we created nine years ago and have been nurturing since. Even though this is the best possible situation for us, it still feels disconcerting. Like sending your kid away to college or something. But that's something we need to deal with ourselves. And I'd be remiss if I didn't mention that I know there will be people who'll consider us to be sellouts. Not many, but some. Fortunately, we've already heard some of that—each time one of us writes something even remotely critical of another Black person (particularly a Black male), we hear everything from "VSB is controlled by Zionists" to "them niggas were bought by NBC"—so we're used to it. (Young, 2017a, para. 17)

Instead of the enclave's insularity, the discourse on *VSB* shifted to a counterpublic where writers were aware that their readers might no longer be only other Black folks. The comments section on *VSB* is now managed by Gizmodo, with users required to create a new account and username with Kinja to post comments.[17] This was a small shift on the surface, but the carefully crafted community that Jackson and Young created changed.

Long before the move to the *Root* and G/O Media, the blog was a progressive site. In writing about women and relationships, they recognized the humanity of their partners. They often joked about men's shortcomings as partners, not to absolve themselves but to push themselves and their readers to do better. While Young and Jackson never named *VSB* a Black feminist site, the arguments produced by both the writers and the community of readers regularly featured Black feminist rhetoric. Posts contained interrogations of patriarchy and misogyny, particularly as they relate to the Black community. Young carefully critiques his relationship with his masculinity and how coming to understand his male privilege has shaped who he is in his relationships. Jackson, often known for offering posts on music and popular culture, also provides a steady hand in increasingly progressive Black feminist writing. For example, a December 4, 2013, post on *VSB* written by Panama Jackson is titled "7 Reasons Why Men Should Watch Scandal according to an Actual Man." Jackson challenges cis, straight, Black men to accept that they may enjoy some of the same things their women partners may enjoy. Patriarchy dictates that the norms and desires of men and women must differ. Jackson's humorous argument about a popular network television series is rooted in the idea that strict adherence to hegemonic gender norms is harmful to men and women in creating equitable and healthy romantic relationships. As he explains,

> The only reason you probably refuse to watch it is because all the women love it. Which is a stupid reason. It's a good show, if not entertaining. Choosing not to watch it because women swoon too much over it is perhaps the worst of the reasons not to check it out. You could attack the premise. You could attack the side-piece ness of nearly EVERYBODY on the show (seriously, I've counted at least 4 sidepieces on this show . . . even the sidepieces have sidepieces), the lack of realism at times, Quinn (who we all want to die), Liv's wardrobe consisting of only white, or maybe it just ain't your thing. But for all of those, you'd have to watch it to know. And you're not doing it. Besides we like tons of sh*t that women hate and tolerate because they care about us. (P. Jackson, 2014)

Jackson pushes for reciprocity in relationships. This form of Black feminist rhetoric recognizes patriarchy as oppressive to both men and women. Men are involved in this discourse, not merely as allies for women, but as advocates for themselves.

Over the years, Young and Jackson, two very smart brothas, also opened their platform and developed a lineup of other writers who blogged regularly on the site, mostly very smart *sistas*. The community of *VSB* has been a learning space for readers and the bloggers as we see both Young and Jackson become more vocal about misogyny and misogynoir. As *VSB*'s popularity grew, Young and Jackson created careers in writing and public speaking, often teaming up with Black feminist thinkers for book talks and other public events. In their public talks and books and on the blog, they promote Black women, ensuring their writing does not overshadow the work upon which they build many of their insights. In a follow-up to the controversial September 2017 piece by Young, he cites prominent Black feminist writers and thinkers like bell hooks and Kimberlé Crenshaw but also contemporary writers like Brittney Cooper and Jamilah Lemieux, saying, "I was uncomfortable with the positive attention this received. There are people who've written and worked much more extensively on this topic . . . all better equipped than I am to articulate the intersections between race, class, gender, and sex" (Young, 2018b).

Digital Black feminism creates complicated allegiances between Black men and Black women wherein a blog titled *Very Smart Brothas* can be a conduit for enclaved Black feminist discourse. Black women did not create *VSB*, nor is it run by Black women, yet this does not make it devoid of digital Black feminist rhetoric. Not all content on the blog is widely feminist. Many posts never deal with gender, and some do so in ways most would not regard as feminist. Nevertheless, one principle of digital Black feminism is a willingness to form complicated allegiances, finding accomplices in the struggle for liberation without a purity test. Digital Black feminists are building allegiances online with Black men interested in unsettling patriarchy even when they may still struggle with their investment in it.

*VSB* provides two opportunities to witness the complicated allegiances of digital Black feminists. First, Jackson and Young's site fosters community dialogue in ways that mirror the virtual beauty shop. Though it did not begin as a Black feminist enclave, the bloggers and their community members hold space for this discursive community. The two cultivate a blog where they are not the sole experts or arbiters of truth. As a virtual beauty shop, their comment structure intentionally undermines what Collins calls the "Eurocentric masculinist knowledge validation process" (Collins, 1989, p. 751). As Collins explains, a Black feminist knowledge-validation process requires incorporating interactive networks of dialogue, including call-and-response, as tools of fostering knowledge. Rather than singular authoritative figures, Black feminists produce knowledge through discussion. The comments section of many blogs can be a place of harsh insults and hate speech. As Young and Jackson demonstrate in their blog's early years, it can also be a productive site to create knowledge as a community. They make use of the long tradition of call-and-response in Black oral culture. Just as congregants appraise a preacher's words in church, so too do readers make appraisals on the content of Young and Jackson's posts and on how they deliver it. The dialogue in the comments is among peers. So the first allegiance is with Young and Jackson as allies and accomplices to the Black women they name as the Black feminist thinkers who guide their work. *VSB* as a feminist enclave demonstrates the complicated allegiances within digital Black feminist thought.

The second example of complicated allegiances connects to the digital world in which the bloggers establish this principle. The inspiration for this principle happened long before the advent of blogging. However, it is online where the need for such allegiances becomes so pronounced and becomes a central tenant of digital Black feminist thought. Within the early blogosphere, most bloggers hosted their own sites, eventually drawing a big enough readership that some could solicit advertising. As I discuss more in chapter 5, blogging allowed digital Black feminists to begin branding themselves and their content in a way that led to more avenues of income. However, for many who rose in popularity, this meant partnering with large media sites and selling content to other publishing venues. Within these arrangements, as we see with *VSB*, there is a trade-off. For *VSB*, Young's and Jackson's content got a much bigger audience. The two received opportunities to have their writing showcased on a national stage. Articles like Young's (2017b) "Straight Black Men Are the White People of Black People" and Jackson's (P. Jackson, 2017) "How Trump Ruined My Relationship with My White Mother"[18] reached audiences different from the typical *VSB* reader. But with this extension to a broader audience, they lost the enclave they built so meticulously, trading it for the opportunities a thriving counterpublic provides. Unlike enclaves, counterpublics utilize different rhetorical strategies to reclaim space in the public sphere and host intergroup dialogue. The two formed a complicated allegiance with a media company, recognizing the benefit of their relationship with their new media partners all the while aware of fans' perceptions and their ability to control the dialogue on the site.

Digital Black feminism is deeply practical and much less focused on a litmus test for participation. Using the space that they have and the people they have relationships with, digital Black feminists advance causes they care about on platforms that may not belong to them. They acquired this practicality from their feminist foremothers, who frequently made choices and decisions based on what they could most readily do to impact the lives of those they touched and cared about daily. They suffered in silence working in white homes where white employers shamed them for their Blackness, forced them outside to use the bathroom, and prevented them from eating at the same table where they served. They did this to save money, put their kids through school, and hope that they had a different life. They dealt with husbands who sometimes treated their relationships as an opportunity to hold power within an otherwise powerless existence, fighting alongside those same men for racial justice. Digital Black feminism finds the same utility in the revolutionary pragmatism of complicated allegiances. Things do not always look the way we want them to look. Gaining access to bigger audiences and more stable homes for your work may require partnering with corporate media companies who profit from your labor, and our accomplices in the struggle may be very smart brothas.

## A Dialectic of Self and Community Interests

Three Black women—Patrisse Cullors, Alicia Garza, and Opal Tometi—created the hashtag #BlackLivesMatter. Garza first wrote the phrase in a Facebook post after the death of Trayvon Martin in 2013. In 2014, after police officer Darren Wilson killed a young Black man, Michael Brown, in Ferguson, Missouri, Cullors turned Black Lives Matter into a hashtag, and Tometi helped transform it into an organizing platform online (Cobb, 2016). After deploying #BlackLivesMatter, the three continued their activist work, meeting with politicians, releasing policy statements, and organizing around issues of injustice around the country. Buoyed by the popularity of the hashtag, regional organizations emerged to work locally on racial justice, some connected to Black Lives Matter,[19] others to organizations under the umbrella of the Movement for Black Lives,[20] and many more functioning independently. History teaches us that even as Black women do the work of social movements, the fight for rights for

Black folks has traditionally focused on men. Black feminist activists and scholars have always worked for civil rights and freedom from oppression in the U.S. For much of this fight, though, their work has been ignored, co-opted, or further maligned. Despite the sexism rampant in many factions of the civil rights movement, Black women have always contributed to the struggle, often using their platforms to advocate for the rights of Black men. Antilynching campaigns, for example, were led by Black feminist activists like Ida B. Wells-Barnett, who used her writing to advocate for Black men, hoping that Black women would gain residual benefit. In doing this work, other groups also co-opted their labor. As Treva Lindsey (2020) explains, white antirape activists in the 1970s used Black women's strategies from the 1800s to make their claims. The #MeToo movement in 2017 initially overlooked the work of Black activist Tarana Burke, and Black trans women like Marsha P. Johnson are often left out of the history of queer activism by mainstream gay and lesbian organizations. In the current movement to #DefundThePolice, Lindsey insists, "To re-center the lives and labor of Black women, girls and femmes in the current debate about #DefundThePolice isn't merely about recognition; it's about ensuring that we don't render them as no one" (Lindsey, 2020, para. 10). Digital Black feminists have recognized the need for a different strategy, prioritizing a public dialectic of self-and community interests as a defense mechanism against the tendency for Black women's physical and emotional needs to be ignored during the fight for Black lives.

Black feminist writers have always recognized the hypocrisy of those who would have Black women do the work of advocating for Black men without reciprocation. However, bloggers position negotiating this dialectic as a necessary component of freedom. Before Black feminists dealt with the public killings of Black men and boys endlessly circulated on social media and in mainstream news, they had created enclaves online. Blogging prepared them for the onslaught with the ability to stand in solidarity with their brothers while demanding the space to care for themselves. While platforms like Twitter provide publicity and are well suited for engagement in counterpublic discourse meant to direct debate toward the dominant group, the blogosphere of the early 2000s provided a space for digital Black feminists to hone complicated and controversial arguments with a veil of protection.

In 2016, political analyst, television personality, and professor of political science Melissa Harris-Perry's departure from her MSNBC weekend show prompted shock and praise within the Black blogosphere. Harris-Perry, who once wrote for several prominent online blogs, often used her television platform to promote young Black writers, bloggers, scholars, and Twitter aficionados as experts on politics, digital culture, activism, housing, education, and more. Bloggers and other Black feminist thinkers recognized the end of Harris-Perry's show as consequential for their community of public scholarship. She placed their online work within the national spotlight of cable news. However, during the 2016 campaign, Harris-Perry's weekend show on MSNBC was preempted to feature a panel program focused on the campaign season events. This new panel noticeably featured few regular Black guests. Their absence was especially notable because MSNBC promoted multiple Black anchors and commentators to prominent roles on the network during Obama's years in the White House. After weeks of speculation regarding the show's future, Harris-Perry confirmed rumors of her departure by releasing a letter to her bosses at the network. In the letter, she wrote, "I will not be used as a tool for their purposes. . . . I am not a token, mammy or little brown bobblehead. I am not owned by [NBC executives] or MSNBC. I love our show. I want it back" (Byers, 2016). She condemned the network for what appeared to be an intentional demographic shift in hosts during the 2016 election cycle that excluded Black journalists.

Harris-Perry did not need to explain her assertion that "she would not serve as a mammy," as she had already done so while blogging for the *Root* years before. In a 2008 blog post on the *Root*, Harris-Perry explains that the mammy myth allowed "Americans in the North and South to ignore the brutality of slavery. These women masked their true thoughts and personalities to gain a modicum of security for themselves and their families. The Mammy monument was meant to display Black women as the faithful, feisty, loyal servants of white domesticity" (Harris-Perry, 2008, para. 5). In subsequent interviews, Harris-Perry made clear that she was not accusing her former employer of intentionally trying to harm her because of her race. Instead, we should read her accusations of tokenism as a broader indictment of an industry that uses Black faces on the screen as a salve without more carefully interrogating the racism and misogyny of political coverage and political news more broadly. In sending the letter and leaving the network, Harris-Perry navigated a careful balance between her career interest and labor and the impact of her departure for her community.

Harris-Perry's decision to protect herself reflects the kind of nuanced public consideration of self and community that Black feminist bloggers worked through in their online writing a decade earlier. In that same 2008 blog post where Harris-Perry described the mammy, she explored the racial and gendered politics between then senators Hillary Rodham Clinton and Barack Obama during the 2008 Democratic primary campaign. In 2008, Clinton struggled to win over Black women voters. Harris-Perry in "Hillary's Scarlett O'Hara Act" explains that Black women overwhelmingly supported Barack Obama, not because they chose their race over their gender, but because Clinton's "ascendance was not a liberating symbol." She argues that "privileged white women, attached at the hip to their husband's power and influence, have been complicit in Black women's oppression. Many African American women are simply refusing to play Mammy to Hillary" (Harris-Perry, 2008). Harris-Perry explains that white America continually asks Black women to play mammy—providing them comfort and escape from accountability.

In 2016, Black women who chose not to play mammy to Clinton came out at a higher percentage than any other demographic group to support her second bid for the White House. Black women's support for Clinton in 2016 and lack of support for her in 2008 were motivated by the same principle, a dialectic of self and community needs. Operating with a dialectic of self and community needs means that Black women's support for political leaders is a carefully calculated and strategic vote centered on self and community protection and care. Political parties and leaders are not saviors; Black women know that the only folks interested in saving Black women are ourselves. The shift in support was not an erasure of misgivings about Clinton. Instead, many recognized Clinton as someone with whom they could now form a complicated allegiance. They also recognized that this allegiance was a means to protect themselves and their communities from a far worse fate. Harris-Perry, in her blog post, her letter, and her departure from MSNBC, was articulating the importance of self-care.

Audre Lorde wrote about self-care as a resistance strategy, as self-preservation, and as ultimately political. As she describes, self-care is not merely about remembering to do a kind thing for oneself. For Black women, self-care is a political decision to prioritize one's health, safety, and care in a space where you are under assault. When Harris-Perry ended her show, she referred to it as "our show," acknowledging that the decision carried consequences for herself and the many Black folks for whom her show was a platform and source of information. In February and March of 2016, multiple bloggers writing for the *Root* and subsidiaries discussed the importance of Harris-Perry's show and her public decision to part ways with MSNBC. Tracey Ross penned an essay titled "An Open Letter to Melissa Harris-Perry from a Grateful Student." In it, she explains, "Compromising your show format would have been tantamount to allowing a university to ban the books on your syllabus. The end of your show is a huge loss to those of us who are hungry to learn, working for progressive change, or are increasingly disappointed by the media landscape, and cable and network news in particular" (Ross, 2016, para. 8). Harris-Perry's unwillingness to compromise on her show was a personal decision about her career and well-being but also a decision that spoke to an entire community's relationship with tokenism and compromise.

Even when bloggers did not frame their work as activism, many viewed blogging as civic engagement for themselves and their readers. As a practice of critical thinking, blogging provides the space for writers to work through ideas before the polish. It affords an enclave to challenge ideas and arguments before the work is complete. Even bloggers whose sites are public and who seek a large following create boundaries for participation with their content. At the time of Michael Brown's death, on her pop culture and humor blog, blogger Luvvie Ajayi warned against the type of comments she would not tolerate in her space. When posting about Brown, she was vigilant about ensuring users could not use her posts to disparage or disrespect him or the people of Ferguson. At one point that year, she removed herself entirely from the media storm and the public pain of racism, announcing she would be leaving her site temporarily and with it the labor of producing anything for anyone but herself. Ajayi recognized her role in providing thoughtful commentary and hosting a place for people to grieve together, yet she also created firm boundaries to protect herself, insisting that she as a person was as valuable as the work she produced for her community. Digital Black feminists first articulated this dialectic of self and community needs in the blogosphere where they owned "the shops." This principle now extends beyond the enclaved space of the Black feminist blogosphere.

Since the emergence of #BlackLivesMatter, Black feminist writers and activists like Feminista Jones worked tirelessly to ensure Black women were not erased from social media campaigns, creating hashtags like #YouOKSis.[21] The death of Sandra Bland in police custody propelled #SayHerName to the top of Twitter's trending topics as Black women once again reminded the country that to be a Black woman is to fight for racial justice that often is not extended to us. When women and gender nonbinary folks saw themselves excluded from #BlackLivesMatter, Black feminist activists online adjusted their strategies. In 2020, when massive protests erupted following the deaths of Ahmaud Arbery, George Floyd, and Breonna Taylor, the fight for Black lives again retook center stage after being muted during the authoritarian Trump presidency. When police arrested the men who killed Arbery and the state brought charges against the offers who killed George Floyd, mainstream news outlets shifted coverage away from the ongoing protests. On digital platforms like TikTok, Twitter, and Instagram, people continued to say the name of Breonna Taylor, insisting she not be forgotten. Black feminists online led protests, wrote op-eds, and petitioned government officials such as Daniel Cameron, the attorney general in Kentucky, who abdicated his responsibility to charge officers for Taylor's death. Speaking alongside Taylor's family, activist Tamika Mallory addressed Cameron, a Black man, directly, saying, "You are a coward, you are a sellout, and you were used by the system to harm your own mama. Your own Black mama." She went on, "I thought about him saying he's a Black man. I thought about the ships that went into Fort Monroe and Jamestown with our people on them over 400 years ago and how there were also Black men on those ships that were responsible for bringing our people over here. Daniel Cameron is no different than the sellout negroes that sold our people into slavery" (Telusma, 2020). In her public speech, Mallory addresses an all too familiar situation, Black men not working to extend rights to Black cis and trans women and gender nonbinary folks. Refusing to take a back seat any longer, Black women continued to march and fight for justice, demanding that Black women like Breonna Taylor not be ignored and that Black men not be complicit in our pain. And as Black women continue to march and fight for justice, they demand that Black women like Breonna Taylor not be ignored and that Black men not be complicit in their pain.

Digital Black feminists organized online to work toward a world where they receive reciprocity for their constant support of Black men. They drew upon complicated allegiances in their politics and demanded agency over their bodies. At the same time, they insisted on the ability to rest, revive themselves, provide to themselves the care required to resist and to remain alive. Visible practices of care for digital Black feminists are tools in the struggle against misogynoir. Though she names herself a product of hip-hop feminism, Harris-Perry's departure from cable news, her announcement of it, and the reaction to it are all mitigated by digital Black feminism's relationship to digital tools and culture. Digital culture compels Black women to pursue a dialectic of self and community interests and provides the platforms where they can sit with the complexity of these choices. A dialectic of self and community interest is a principle that builds upon each of the others described in this chapter to insist that Black women's needs are at the center of the struggle for freedom. Black feminists craft each of the principles outlined in this chapter in the blogosphere. Blogging served as a medium to distribute new principles; the relationship Black feminist thinkers formed with blogging shifted their principles as well.

While principles of agency, complicated allegiances, and self-care have been a part of Black feminist discourses of the past, digital culture provides a new urgency and priority. The virtual beauty shop is more than a site where Black feminists work. The shop's affordances and tools impact how digital Black feminists form new strategies and find methods for deployment. The blogosphere provided a unique environment for Black feminist thinkers to work out ideas, cultivate community, and create a safe harbor. Blogging opened the doors to new possibilities in Black feminist thought. Like blogging, older mediums like the voice, the pen, and the typewriter have contributed to the Black feminist praxis. Now that we have considered blogging as an origin point for the virtual beauty shop and Black feminist technoculture, I analyze Black feminist praxis through mediums of the past and newer platforms like Twitter and Instagram.

# 4

# Digital Black Feminist Praxis, or Mavis Beacon Teaches Typing

When I was around ten years old, Mavis Beacon taught me to type. Every day after school, my lessons began on my family's shared computer. I placed my fingers on the keys and started where I left off the day before, checking to see if my words per minute and percentage of words typed correctly had improved. Each day, Mavis Beacon provided me lessons and activities that strengthened my muscle memory and taught my fingers the agility needed to move about the keyboard with fewer and fewer errors. On the cover of the CD-ROM case, Mavis Beacon wore a yellow suit and white pearls. Her hair was slicked back into a neat bun. This Black woman was my typing teacher, and she was the expert typing teacher for many other little Black girls in the late 1980s and 1990s. The 1989 issue of *Compute!* described Mavis Beacon this way: "Mavis Beacon lets you work through a series of lessons, according to your own ability, with the goal of becoming a touch-typist. With the keyboard, the input device of many computer programs, typing skills are more important now than they have ever been" (Randall, 1989, p. 70). For Black feminists of a certain age, she was also one of the few public images of Black computing expertise of our youth.

A generation of Black feminists started their relationship with digital technology with an image crafted by a company to sell software. Mavis Beacon was not a real person. Instead, the image used to market the typing software was that of a retired model.[1] Still, Beacon normalized for at least some little Black girls that a Black woman has space in this new world of computing, whether she was "real" or not. Her typing course provided a skill set that became a necessary component of digital Black feminist praxis. Her manufactured image is also instructive in how digital Black feminists form their relationship to technology. Typing, a productive skill for a new economy, was pitched to the public by an image of a Black woman who lives only in the imagination of the software developers and not by the actual Black women whose technical skills have long served the economic needs of others.

While typing was long considered an appropriate profession for Black women serving in secretarial positions in the mid and late twentieth century, learning to type on the computer for Black girls in the 1990s was not as preparation to be a secretary. Typing, in a world of home computers, was no longer the work of an assistant. Instead, typing was quickly becoming a required skill for all working professionals, content creators, and writers. There is agency in typing an essay filled with your own thoughts. To be able to share those thoughts online was a gift provided by Mavis Beacon, at least in part. However, before digital Black feminists began writing in the blogosphere, penning Twitter threads, and developing long-form essays online, Black feminist orators made the transition to writing their thoughts in the form of essays, news articles, folk stories, and memoirs.

The voice as a form of Black vernacular technological creativity remains a powerful tool for those once held in bondage. Rayvon Fouché (2006) describes Black vernacular technological creativity as the redeployment, reconception, and recreation of language by Black folks across the diaspora that "results from resistance to existing technology and strategic appropriations of the material and symbolic power and energy of technology" (p. 641). These discursive strategies are resistant responses and technological appropriations that are politically motivated and culturally embedded. However, time-based media, like speech, are limited by their extension into time. The voice and the spoken word favor cultures and systems of stability, community, and tradition,[2] while writing provides a distance between the technology and the body, an extension into both space and time. Writing is a mechanism by which Black women can assert agency in the telling of their own stories.

Black feminist thinkers in the early Americas adopted literacy as a tool to extend their advocacy beyond where their voices could reach. However, the relationship of the Black feminist to the pen is marked initially by the prohibition of its use. White persons in North Carolina and across the country believed that if enslaved persons learned to write, insurrection and rebellion would follow.[3] Passed by the General Assembly of the State of North Carolina at the Session of 1830–31, the

Act to Prevent All Persons from Teaching Slaves to Read or Write reads as follows:

> Whereas the teaching of slaves to read and write, has a tendency to excite dis-satisfaction in their minds, and to produce insurrection and rebellion, to the manifest injury of the citizens of this State. Therefore, be it enacted by the General Assembly of the State of North Carolina, and it is hereby enacted by the authority of the same, That any free person, who shall hereafter teach, or attempt to teach, any slave within the State to read or write, the use of figures excepted, or shall give or sell to such slave or slaves any books or pamphlets, shall be liable to indictment in any court of record in this State having jurisdiction thereof. (Act to Prevent All Persons, 1830, p. 15)

In the antebellum period, humanity itself became tied to the ability to tell one's own story via the written word, thus signaling the importance of memoirs and diaries for free Black women following slavery (Atwater, 2009). To be fully human in that period equated to having the ability to write one's own story. As Lu explains, "Natural rights claims to freedom were also constrained by heavy emphasis on formal education and literacy. Freedom had to be meticulously taught and diligently learned, rather than merely recognized in all human beings. This clarification held African Americans to standards of reading, writing, and speaking. According to both white and Black voices, formal education and literacy was required to both understand freedom's meaning in America and, ultimately, argue for the deliverance of freedom for emancipated slaves" (J. H. Lu, 2017, p. 24). Writing was a way to resist illiteracy as a tool of confinement. The act of writing separates the author's ideas from her body and potentially forces a sort of "objectivity" that orality and oral cultures do not. Writing requires an imagined audience different from those who sit immediately before you. The extension of thoughts using the pen allows us to consider how our ideas live beyond our bodies. For Black feminist writers, the relationship to the pen unbinds their words to the public gaze in an immediate way. Writing provides both a space of quiet reflection and the opportunity to present arguments to an audience without the presence of a physical body, which in the case of Black women, is too often ignored and marginalized.

While Black folks have maintained their relationship to oral culture during and following enslavement in the U.S., the embrace of writing is a significant shift for Black feminist thought. The tools we use to write can function in pursuit of freedom or as a cage that further restricts ideas and freedoms. For example, literacy as an implicit requirement of citizenship dismisses oral cultures as inferior. Likewise, the typewriter's adoption yields a relationship with a new tool that is simultaneously liberating and confining. In her book *Black Macho and the Myth of the Superwoman*, Michele Wallace describes Black women involved in the civil rights movement. Typing was a skill Black women honed and performed as a part of their work in the shadows of the movement (Wallace, 1999). They were responsible for an inordinate amount of typing, coffee making, and housework. Relegation to typists and housekeepers signaled their lack of import and value to their male counterparts. Those with power did not consider typing to be a skill of a leader or a thought maker. Instead, typing was a tool to support those who produced knowledge. Anthropologist and folklorist Zora Neale Hurston began her writing career as a typist for her future patron Charlotte Osgood Mason. She hated typing and ultimately was not very good at it (Taylor, 2019). Being viewed as a typist devalued the intellectual work that Hurston sought to have funded, but it provided an entry point to a relationship with her future patron. The typewriter served as a technology of both entry and restriction.

For digital Black feminists, typing *online* yields a new relationship to the practice. Xennials (older millennials) and younger members of Generation X came of age at a time when typing was an increasingly desirable skill to hone, in school or on one's own. With the public's introduction to home computing, we spent our formative years in middle and high school working in computer labs and libraries. We used word processors or school-owned computers to type college applications and began texting on flip phones before encountering QWERTY keyboards on smartphones in our twenties. Xennials are not "digital natives" per se but came of age during the transition from typing up handwritten ideas to *forming* ideas on the computer. This transition signals another critical shift in the practice of creating Black feminist thought.

A specific kind of writing takes place in digital spaces. To type ideas rather than write them and then transfer them to the typewriter or word processor later means that we intertwine our thoughts with keys and screens. The entire concept of revision changes when typing. You back-space and delete rather than cross out to revise. Your screen has multiple open tabs connecting you immediately to your audience and endless pos-sibilities for research. Writing using digital tools changes our relationship to knowledge production. While studies suggest that typing on a com-puter is perhaps *faster* than handwriting (C. M. "Lin" Brown, 1988), few recent studies consider what other affordances online writing provides to touch typists as they produce their work. Further, we have little knowl-edge of the relationship the writer has with the actual activity of writing online and what this relationship yields in the way of content produced.

In this chapter, I consider technology's relationship to Black feminist users' praxis. I begin with the affordances and constraints of the tech-nologies employed by Black feminist thinkers in their lives and their praxis. As Florini (2019) explains,

> Often scholarly attention to technological affordances focuses on how the materiality of technology—such as interface or design choices—shapes user behavior, an approach that has been criticized by some as verging on technological determinism. I embrace Peter Nagy and Gina Neff's concept of *imagined affordances*, which highlights how affordances arise 'between users' perceptions, attitudes, and expectations; between the ma-teriality and functionality of technologies; and between the intentions and perceptions of designers.' The term thus captures the contingent and shifting nature of affordances as well as the influence users have in the emergence of affordances (pp. 5–6).

To consider the praxis of digital Black feminism, I shift from the content of what they produce to a critical examination of *how* Black feminist writers use tools of technology, how they relate to those tools, and what impact those tools have on their process. Tools and technology change rapidly, reminding us that while it is essential to mark new platform affordances, it is perhaps most valuable for scholars of communication to consider what remains constant in human use of technology. I focus on the rela-tional quality between the authors and the tools rather than detailing each platform's specific affordances. This chapter compares platforms like Twitter, Instagram, or Facebook to the pen, the voice, and the typewriter, noting when new communicative needs arise and how shifts in use track with cultural and ideological shifts. By turning our focus to Black feminist praxis, I highlight the relationship Black women form with their tools and the relationship Black women have to their work.

I focus on six Black feminist writers' work, three whose work emerged in the twentieth century and three whose work emerges online in the twenty-first century. Zora Neale Hurston, Anna Julia Cooper, and Ida B. Wells-Barnett approach their work differently based on their differentiated training in anthropology, philosophy, and journalism, respectively. Hurston writes as a folklorist from the South, careful to avoid the "race work" so many Black authors were known for at the time. Wells-Barnett approaches her work as an activist and journalist, bringing light to crimes and violence committed against Black folks in America. Cooper, an educator and scholar, writes about sexualized racism often for a white audience. In the twenty-first century, I look to the work of Jamilah Lemieux, Luvvie Ajayi, and Feminista Jones. Lemieux is a journalist, consultant, and acclaimed writer and editor working at numerous well-known magazines and newspapers. Jones, a social worker, digital activist, author, and sought-after speaker, gives talks on topics ranging from feminism to sex work and social media. Ajayi began writing a small lifestyle and humor blog whose popularity landed her multiple book deals, podcasts, and an online business in brand marketing. Each cultivated a strong following on multiple social media platforms and has transformed their online audiences into opportunities beyond the digital space. We have access to both the public writing and private papers (letters and diaries) of many Black feminist thinkers of the twentieth century thanks to archivists' preservation work. From these documents, we can glean a difference in how they privately reflect on their relationship to technology and the public work they produce as Black feminist intellectuals. However, for those writing online in the twenty-first century, public and private praxis are in the very same document and on the very same app. Given this reality, close readings provide more insight into how these authors navigate their public and private selves and whether such a distinction holds firm in a digital era.

Studying these Black feminist thinkers—writing at different times, with differing audiences and differing styles—provides insight into the praxis of Black feminist thought. It also provides a way to understand how their relationships with technology might impact said praxis. For

Hurston, typing is a constraint on writing; however, Mavis Beacon provided many digital Black feminists a relationship to typing that yields a connection with machines and computing different from our experience with the pen. Feeling liberated typing on the phone or computer, if only briefly, opens possibilities for what we create within their parameters.

## Capturing

In the book *Barracoon*, Zora Neale Hurston interviews Cudjo Lewis, one of the last known survivors of the transatlantic slave trade. In the 1927 interview, he details his *capture* and life in the U.S. that followed (Hurston & Miles, 2018). Raised in Eatonville, Florida, Hurston traveled back to her hometown and across the South to *capture* Black life in the early part of the twentieth century. In her autobiography, she *captured* pieces of her own life. The word *capture* is always indicative of power. Who is in a position to *capture*? What do they choose to *capture*, and ultimately, what becomes of the *capturer* and the *captured*? Patricia Hill Collins's matrix of domination reminds us of the dominant group's long-standing prerogative to control the *capture* and distribution of images of Blackness and Black women. Still, the activity of capturing, curating, and making available one's life in words and images also shows the complicated relationship Black feminists have to the activity of capture in their praxis.

Hurston's relationship to capture is one of freedom and constraint. Bound by her relationship to her patron, Hurston is captured by her patron's desires and whims yet also afforded the financial freedom to produce work that dispels the notion of the Black subject as "tragically colored." Hurston, while traveling in the South with her camera and pen, captures images of Black culture. Her journey back to Eatonville is a visit home and social scientific research. Hurston completes this work as a commissioned project by her patron, Charlotte Osgood Mason, whom she referred to as Godmother. "Godmother" required her "godchildren" to record "all things financial, domestic, nutritional, and digestive. . . . Every penny spent, every piece of linen purchased, every calorie consumed, each bodily waste emitted" (Taylor, 2019, p. 86). In her letters to her patron, Hurston provides effusive praise of Mason, writing, "It is you who gives out life and light and we who receive. I wish I knew how many you have dragged from everlasting unseeing to heaven" (Hurston, 2002, p. 231). This flattery continues for years during their patron-beneficiary relationship, with Hurston's devotion evident in their correspondence. Mason's patronage of both Hurston and her onetime friend Langston Hughes came with control of how the images, both literal and figurative, that they captured could be used and distributed and steep consequences for violating her wishes.

In letters to their shared patron, Hurston and Hughes debate ownership of the play *Mule Bone*. *Mule Bone* is based on a short story Hurston wrote in 1925, though it has attribution to both Hurston and Langston Hughes (Taylor, 2019). Hurston unsuccessfully attempts to sway Mason, speaking to the severity and urgency of Hughes's actions. Hurston provides her account of the play's origins, arguing against her onetime close friend and ally Hughes. According to Taylor (2019), Hurston initially defers to Mason as an arbiter and decision maker in her and Hughes's disagreement. Mason insisted Hurston abandon the project and instead move forward with the more *important* work of writing the book she commissioned. Since the play was the product of interviews and accounts she captures on the trip to Eatonville, paid for by Mason, Hurston acquiesced in her correspondence with Mason. While she certainly did not let go of the conflict forever, Hurston, like many Black writers reliant on the patronage of white women and men, had signed away full autonomy of her work product.

Within the confines of her patronage, Hurston used the praxis of capture to produce folk stories that move away from viewing Black life as wrought with hardship and peril. Much of her work went unrecognized at the time of its completion. *Barracoon* went unpublished until 2018, and the play she battled for control of with Hughes was not staged until the 1990s. Yet her anthropological and folkloric work is a model for researchers today. Hurston's work captured the humor, the banality, the joy, and the irreverence of Black life. In her essay "Characteristics of Negro Expression," Hurston writes the following:

> Negro dancing is dynamic suggestion. No matter how violent it may appear to the beholder, every posture gives the impression that the dancer will do much more. For example, the performer flexes one knee sharply, assumes a ferocious face mask, thrusts the upper part of the body forward

with clenched fists, elbows taut as in hard running or grasping a thrust-
ing blade. That is all. But the spectator himself adds the picture of fero-
cious assault, hears the drums and finds himself keeping time with the
music and tensing himself for the struggle. It is compelling insinuation.
That is the very reason the spectator is held so rapt. He is participating in
the performance himself—carrying out the suggestions of the performer.
(Hurston, 2000a, pp. 60–61)

Hurston's literature does the same. It *compels* the reader. We keep time
alongside Joni and Tea Cake.[4] She shifts our ideas about Black life and
recognizes the pain and hardship without ever allowing them to be our
defining features. We find ourselves using the characters she creates
to understand the fullness of Black life and perhaps ourselves as well.
Using the camera and pen, Hurston points her lens outward, using eth-
nographic work to tell the story of Black life in the South. However, for
digital Black feminists, the lens must first point at themselves before it
looks into the world.

## The Self-ie

*Capture* takes on a different meaning when the camera faces inward.
Selfies and self-capture provide a semblance of agency, regardless of
whether they provide material and consequential shifts in the balance
of social, economic, or political power (Tiidenberg, 2018). Tiidenberg
(2018) defines selfies as photographic, digitally rendered representations
of self. She describes selfies as simultaneously performance, a mode of
interactivity, work, and tools we use to think. The literal and metaphorical move to place cameras on the front of the smartphone changes the
possibilities of capture as an act of curation and construction of self.
Black feminist writers have always seen the self at the center of research.
No work is devoid of the researcher's experiences or biases. Black
feminist epistemology views acknowledgment of subjectivity and posi-
tionality as valuable. The connection between the Black feminist writer
and the community she writes for and about is not a problem to be
resolved; it is a feature of the work. However, this does not fully explain
the shift in praxis required to do Black feminist work online wherein
one must capture their personal life as a part of outward-facing public

work. The selfie and the ubiquity of self-capture online force a reconciliation for digital Black feminists. As proprietors of their virtual beauty shops, they use their public work to push back against institutional and communal acts of oppression. Simultaneously, their envelopment in a digital universe means that their personal lives are also a viewable, shareable, critiqueable part of their public scholarship. Their own life experiences are judged alongside their work, as the curated capture of their lives becomes a work product.

In August of 2018, writer, humorist, podcaster, digital branding entrepreneur, and Black feminist thinker Luvvie Ajayi became the focus of social media ire when she innocuously tweeted about singer Tevin Campbell.[5] Following the death of Aretha Franklin, Black Twitter collectively discussed who could sing in a tribute at her funeral. In a tweet, Ajayi quipped, "Someone suggested Tevin Campbell to sing at Aretha's tribute. Under what rock did they pull that name from?" (Ajayi, 2018a). When Ajayi tweeted the joke, folks on Twitter used the occasion to (1) remind everyone younger than thirty-five that Tevin Campbell was indeed a fantastic singer, (2) mock or ridicule Ajayi for a misstep, or (3) suggest her joke misfired because she is prejudiced against Black Americans. Ajayi first responded, "Tevin Campbell is trending, Lawdt. I KNOW he can blow but I haven't heard his name in awhile. People took my tweet and acted like I called his mama a sinner. I ain't say he can't sing. Folks added all that stuff to that one tweet. Chisos" (Ajayi, 2018b). But as the week went on, the vitriol toward Ajayi, who is of Nigerian descent and has written about herself as Black American for years, seemed wholly disproportionate to the initial tweet. Detractors on Twitter found years-old tweets to provide a thin basis for their critique of her as anti-Black. Ajayi, who has worked on issues of racial justice and continually writes about Black culture, sustained days of "dragging," and "receipt pulling" by some who seemed to be ready to launch a full attack against the comedienne for her potentially misfired joke.

In a digital atmosphere, digital Black feminist writers do not have just one patron to whom they are responsible; they have thousands. As their personal lives online exist alongside their published work, their audience's scrutiny is directed at the misogynoir, patriarchy, and capitalism they write about but also the writers themselves. Digital Black feminists use online writing to capture and shift public sentiment but are likewise bound by people's accessibility to their lives. Ajayi's built her brand on personal insights about television, music, politics, and popular culture. Therefore, as she rose in notoriety, her audience began to see her life as fair game for critique along with her subject matter. Building a successful brand on "side-eye and shade" (https://luvvie.org), Ajayi challenges her readers to offer substantive critiques of those in the public eye. Those same followers and many who do not wish her well were also happy to point the critique back in her direction.

In an Instagram Story in 2019, Ajayi explains to her followers what it is like to have your life as the focus of public attention and scrutiny. She discusses the case of actor Jussie Smollett and his false police report to the Chicago police regarding an alleged hate crime. While the charges were later dropped, Chicago police filed sixteen felony charges against Smollett for filing a false police report about an attack he claimed happened while in town filming a television show. When police dropped the criminal charges, Ajayi celebrated what many saw as the end to an overzealous prosecution. Even if Smollett filed the false report, Ajayi and many others implied that the police department was making an example of the actor in an obvious political and PR move. Ajayi did not dwell on the specifics of the Smollett case in her Instagram Story. Instead, she used the moment to wonder how her followers would respond if a similar charge were levied against her. Ajayi reminded her followers about how public ire has pointed in her direction on multiple occasions.

With her front-facing camera and with unrehearsed honesty, she says, "Maybe this is why I share my story like this," referencing the personal storytelling she can do on platforms like Instagram Stories. In her stories, Ajayi provides glimpses into her day-to-day life. Instagram Stories are a part of the selfie culture that Tiidenberg describes as performative, yet they are unscripted for Ajayi. As she considers the Smollett case, she asks that people remember her as a human, acknowledging that when creatives and writers receive attention for their work, the public views them as characters over which they have authority rather than as whole human people. In this space, it seems, Ajayi feels power over her capture that she does not have on other platforms. On Twitter, a tool she must use to promote her speaking tours, books, and other public projects, her tweets are captured, archived, and used to cause intentional harm to her career. Her old tweets become fodder for debate about her

Blackness or commitment to Black people. As she moves to Instagram Stories, though, Ajayi shifts the dynamics of capture. While Facebook still owns the content created there,[6] her relationship to the practice of creation holds power in this space. An extension of her digital shop, the Instagram Story serves a different role in Ajayi's Black feminist public writing.

## #TheGram

Ajayi shifts between platforms to respond to the new complexities of capture brought by digital storytelling. In 2019, Ajayi further demonstrated her mastery of differentiated platform use to capture and curate her wedding. First, she released a theatrical-style trailer for the event on Twitter. Then she moved to Instagram Stories to post and repost intimate moments of reverence and ratchetry primarily captured by close friends during the ceremonies.[7] Finally, she provided a brief write-up for "friends" on her professional Facebook account. This post included an FAQ about the wedding details and a promise to share more in the coming weeks. Ajayi's Instagram Stories capture joy, family, tradition, and intimacy in ways Facebook and Twitter posts do not. She makes use of platform affordances to move between still and moving images. She plays with vantage points by reposting videos captured by friends. She overlays her commentary atop that of her close friends and family in Instagram Stories, constructing a narrative that encapsulates her feelings and framework for understanding and processing this major life event. While providing this intimate view into her life, she capitalizes on Instagram influencer culture to provide publicity to the Black-owned businesses that she used for event planning, makeup, styling, and DJing her event. Ajayi and her followers use the hashtag #LuvvJones to tag pictures, tweets, and posts about her wedding. This hashtag follows the popular trend of creating a hashtag merging the two people's last names getting married.

Hashtagging is a practice that first emerged on Twitter in 2007. Chris Messina describes the practice as a mechanism to "filter and organize multiple Tweets on a particular topic" (Brock, 2012, p. 534). Brock explains how Black Twitter utilized hashtagging as more than a filtering mechanism. For Black Twitter, hashtags serve as means for a linguistic and cultural community to coalesce and create distance from outsiders. As he explains, the "hashtag serves triple duty as 'signifier,' 'sign,' and, 'signified,' marking as it does the concept to be signified, the cultural context within which the tweet should be understood, and the 'call' awaiting a response" (Brock, 2012, p. 533). Brock's description, which Florini (2013), Freelon et al. (2018), and S. J. Jackson et al. (2020) all take up in their work on Black Twitter, is predicated upon a public performance that the platform requires. Twitter's searchability and trending let hashtags make conversations visible for users to find outside of a single event. For example, #PaulasBestDishes was deployed in 2013 to respond to allegations of racism against television chef Paula Deen. The hashtag turns southern food items into decidedly racist-sounding phrases. The hashtag uses signifyin' to respond to not only Deen but a culture of racism that allows a southern white chef to make millions in drawing on southern Black cuisine while engaging in casual and corporately endorsed racist practices. Coming full circle in 2020, Black Twitter deploys the hashtag #TrueKitchenMenu to mock a Black restaurant owner who verbally berated his customers for twerking and not having decorum in his establishment (which served drinks in used D'ussé bottles while playing trap music). The hashtag brought folks together to signify by creating false menu items that mocked the viral video's respectability tropes. Participation in the hashtag is possible because of the searchability function. Hashtagging provides visibility to in-group discourse.

Like Twitter, Instagram hashtags allow users to search for content, but hashtags like #LuvvJones are not used to reach a broad audience. Some users deployed the hashtag on their private accounts on Instagram, meaning their content would not be searchable on the platform. Instagram further complicates assumptions about hashtag use. Stories disappear after twenty-four hours, rendering hashtags used on stories useless for search and recall even a day later. Instead, hashtags are also part of community discourse and signifyin' practices that do not need to provide the publicity of those deployed on Twitter. Hashtags like #LuvvJones are memory markers for groups that occupy a "space"—either physical, like Ajayi's wedding, or digital, like her Instagram Stories. The hashtag is part of her self-capture. Creating and curating an image of her life that is more intimate and features moments like those mentioned above carry less chance of use by nefarious lurkers and critics. It is a part of her self-performance and functions as a tool in her Black feminist praxis.

Recognizing that her followers consume her private life alongside her public persona, Ajayi curates her stories and memories. She makes use of the affordances of the platform to shift her relationship to the idea of capture. On Instagram Stories, followers cannot pull old content to use against her. She instead takes charge of capture, shifting the relationship to this activity. Her hashtag is a tool to archive the content she creates and that people create about her. It is for her reflection and distribution under her control, from which she may profit. While Facebook owns the data Ajayi produces, she uses hashtagging as praxis to capture her wedding story, control her narrative, and highlight Black businesses she wants to support. Ajayi's relationship with the praxis of capture elucidates some of the possibilities of differentiated platform use for digital Black feminism while highlighting that some similar constraints remain in place from generations past.

Ajayi writes openly as a Black feminist in her book, challenging patriarchal systems and pushing back against stereotypes and prejudice. However, she uses television and celebrity culture to capture the joy and banality of Black life. Like Ajayi's focus on humor and pop culture, much of Hurston's work is intentionally outside the role of race activist. In her 1928 essay "How It Feels to Be Colored Me," Hurston writes,

> I am not tragically colored. There is no great sorrow dammed up in my soul, nor lurking behind my eyes. I do not mind at all. I do not belong to the sobbing school of Negrohood who hold that nature somehow has given them a lowdown dirty deal and whose feelings are all hurt about it. Even in the helter-skelter skirmish that is my life, I have seen that the world is to the strong regardless of a little pigmentation more or less. No, I do not weep at the world—I am too busy sharpening my oyster knife. (Hurston, 2000b, p. 95)

Hurston suggests that her work is unbound to any expectation or preconceived notion based on the "condition" of her race. She is intent on capturing the fullness of Black life yet remains bound financially to her patron. Both writers are at once undertaking the task of capturing Black culture while contending with restrictions of capture on their personal and professional lives. For both Black feminist writers, the praxis of capture is tied to the technologies they rely on to produce their work. Hurston is dependent on patronage for access to the printing and distribution of her writing. However, as Ajayi makes clear, digital tools do not free digital Black feminists from the boundaries of patronage. The accessibility of the audience to the writer's personal life online creates an immediacy of critique and accountability to an audience whose memory is long and often unforgiving. As audiences consume personal images and videos alongside blog posts, news articles, and books, digital Black feminists confront whether their actions, jokes, desires, habits, and hopes align with their work. However, by using digital tools, they curate life on their own terms. Ajayi's relationship to capture on Instagram may not yield power beyond the individual; Facebook will still own her data. Nevertheless, her relationship to capture affords her agency over her image on social media. Digital Black feminists translate this ability to curate images of the self online to new publishing opportunities apart from Twitter or Instagram, producing steady income and respect as professional writers.

## Publishing

For Black feminist writers, publishing is a struggle against institutional measures meant to keep their work from being treated as serious scholarship. In letters to her alma mater Oberlin College in 1941, Anna Julia Cooper demonstrates the challenges of a Black woman attempting to publish academic work (Shilton, 2003). In seeking out an editor for publication of her thesis, nearly sixty years after she wrote it, Cooper initially frames the publication agreement she seeks as a gift to her university, for which she has many pleasant and proud feelings. Cooper writes glowingly about her time at Oberlin. However, as the series of correspondence progresses and Oberlin rebuffs and ignores Cooper, she can no longer write as a benevolent gift giver and instead pleads for recognition. At one point, she even suggests they "just let me disappear from the picture" (A. J. Cooper, 1926), implying that naming her as the author may preclude serious consideration of her work. The act of publishing one's work in the academy is undoubtedly wrought with rejection for anyone. However, for Black women, both in 1941 and in 2021, the added conditions of bias, systemic inequality, and misogynoir mean that publishing is an act of war.

## Persistence, Resistance, and Vulnerability

Cooper's early letters showed deference to her alma mater, her pages filled with gratitude and fond reflections. However, as a student in the late 1800s, she was threatened with firing, was prevented from taking research trips, and had her pay blocked (A. J. Cooper et al., 1998). Her letters do not merely reflect her capacity to find gratitude for her college experience despite the discrimination and challenges she faced. Instead, her words in this correspondence showcase her capacity to publish and circulate a version of reality for an audience eager to consume it. As she writes to convince the institution to publish her thesis and doctoral dissertation, she provides them an image of safe and nondisruptive Black women to support. She does not chastise them for the treatment she endured, nor demand what is rightfully due. Instead, she articulates a case for publishing her work that removes the requirement that her name is attached to it or receive compensation for the publication. Instead, she *altruistically* suggests the publication of her work is purely for the sake of students who may benefit from its reading. Her case for publication reveals the deftness of Cooper's ability to construct rhetorical arguments that dismantle any belief in her perceived inequality as a woman or as a writer.

Cooper's most read work, *A Voice from the South*, was published in 1892. However, so much of her writing before and after its publication remains unpublished. As Shirley Moody-Turner explains,

> Scholarship on *A Voice from the South* has yielded important insights, particularly those focused on Cooper's rhetorical strategies, her contributions to Black feminist thought and intersectional analyses, and her educational theories and praxes. Her larger body of work, however, produced between 1892 until the time of her death in 1964, remains fertile ground for continued scholarship. To advance this work, we must revisit Cooper's archive of published and unpublished writings and revise our notions of what 'counts' as literary production (Moody-Turner, 2019, p. 2).

Cooper frequently used her writing to push for Black women's inclusion in institutions. She publishes and publicizes at the intersection of racism and sexism in the lives of certain Black women. Yet Cooper's rhetorical skill has too often been forgotten. Cooper's life as a scholar and writer may have separated her from the lived reality of many poor Black women, but her Blackness and womanhood created significant challenges as she sought recognition as a scholar.

Using a strategy some call elitist,[8] Cooper highlights those who have "earned" social capital through their education or class status to strip racist actions bare of any ties to arguments about a cultural deficit. Cooper's letters to Oberlin mirror this strategy. Cooper demonstrates that even when Black women meet the artificial criteria of respectability, institutions like Oberlin still reject them. To refuse her gift and require her to plead for help and inclusion make visible the racism that she does not speak of in her letters. Publishing is not for her benefit; it is Black feminist praxis (albeit a form of Black feminist praxis that leaves certain Black women behind). Cooper's relationship to publication is a mechanism to dismantle and unsettle the racist logic of white institutions. Her arguments lay bare the not-so-hidden prejudices of the institution, and her strategy is to disassemble them. Rather than another revisiting of Cooper's rhetorical craft,[9] her letters attune our focus to the praxis of publication and Black feminist's persistence, resistance, and vulnerability in this process.

When a former colleague thanked her in the acknowledgments section of his recently published book, Jamilah Lemieux used Twitter to reflect on the labor of editing and reviewing others' work for publication versus the public gratification of seeing one's work in print. Lemieux is an author, editor, public cultural critic, and political consultant. She pens columns in online magazines and hosts a regular podcast. While sharing her friend and colleague's joy, she tweets about her relationship to the act of publishing, both from the perspective of one who makes it possible for others to do so and as one whose own work is too often sidelined based on said work. As an editor for many years at *Ebony* and NewsOne, Lemieux was responsible for bringing many gifted Black voices to an eager public. She also launched digital platforms for major publications and "moderniz[ed] the[ir] brand voice and identity" (Jamilah Lemieux, n.d.). Writers and public thought leaders like Marc Lamont Hill, Mikki Kendall, and Damon Young have tweeted Lemieux's praise as an editor who provided mentoring to young writers. As Lemieux tweeted in 2019, "I was the first person to edit some of your favorite writers" (Lemieux, 2019b). Providing feedback on their work and improving their craft, the work of the editor in the publishing process is often invisible.

Nevertheless, Lemieux is also a brilliant and award-winning writer in her own right. Her essays have been published in the *Washington Post, Essence, Ebony,* and *Clutch.* Her early writing about criminal sexual assault by R&B singer R. Kelly made her a constant target of online harassment. She has also been on the receiving end of vicious attacks from Fox News for her progressive Black feminist journalism and activism. So her take on publication is informed by her identity as both an editor and a writer. Her relationship to and critique of publishing comes from a unique vantage point as someone situated in distinctly different power relationships with the practice based on her different jobs.

## *Where and When We Publish*

Like Cooper, Lemieux insists that her work be published in channels reserved for professional writers. She operates primarily within the bounds of well-established print and television news and entertainment spaces and at times serves as the editor of those spaces. Lemieux launched a consulting firm in 2018 that offers communication and public relations strategies for individuals and organizations. Based on her professional expertise, she has worked for major political campaigns and nonprofits, providing insights around racial and gender justice. With formal training in her craft, Lemieux has chosen a path wherein her digital praxis troubles the formal institutions of the publishing industry. Her expertise demands inclusion. While necessary for her career, her work also requires that Black feminism not be relegated to the margins. Lemieux expresses the complexity of her relationship to publishing on Twitter, where she is free to post her censored and uncensored thoughts. On Twitter, Lemieux retweets press about her work, links to interviews, and publicizes her podcasts and articles. Unlike many other digital Black feminists, she, as yet, has not used her social media following to charge this audience directly for her work.

Other digital Black feminists have increasingly made the shift to monetize their writing online via Patreon or other paid subscription services or by moving content to platforms they control. In 2019, Luvvie Ajayi created a new platform to host her work and foster deeper connections with her audience, whom she calls LuvvCousins. Ajayi's new platform LuvvNation is a tool for self-promotion, extended networking, and a satellite public filled with those supportive of her work.[10] They have created an affinity group based on their connection to her. The new platform allows Ajayi to publish her work and create an even more devoted following for her future publishing ventures. While the group receives early access to news about her, they mostly use the space to build connections with one another and share online content not created directly by Ajayi but that fits within her brand of humor and snark. Rather than tangling with a publishing industry to convince them of her marketability, she builds her case on a site she controls. As she explained in a tweet on June 29, 2020, "I've been locked out of posting on my Awesomely Luvvie FB [Facebook] page for over a week. The last post on that page is from June 17th. This is also why we CANNOT depend on these social media platforms as the sole way for us to talk to the people who want to hear from us" (Ajayi, 2020). Her labor on LuvvNation is a long-term strategy, which has thus far proved profitable for Ajayi.

Other digital Black feminists are monetizing their writing in nontraditional publishing venues like Patreon. While subscription-based independent publishing provides digital Black feminists immediate access to capital directly from those interested in their work, it is a challenging business model. Feminista Jones's relationship with self-publishing demonstrates the patience required for this type of success and discontent with a system that requires constant production with little profit. As Jones tweets, "I am realizing I get more engagement on Instagram and Facebook than I do via Twitter. I have 10x more followers here, yet those platforms show more clicks and there's more discussion and response to my writing" (Jones, 2019e). The creator of *Gradient Lair*,[11] @thetrudz, responds with screenshots showing how many more likes and shares she gets for tweets where she proposes an idea versus tweets where she asks followers to support the execution of the same idea. As their critiques demonstrate, platforms like Twitter provide users instant access to information and knowledge but little motivation to pursue further engagement that costs them time or money.

Traditional news and magazine publications have run into a similar problem in getting users to subscribe to their print publications' online editions. Marketing firms have researched why metered paywalls do not entice readers to subscribe and pay for the content they are seeking out. Researcher Mary-Katharine Phillips of the digital publishing platform Twipe surveyed more than four thousand newsreaders, finding that more than 50 percent said they would never pay for online access to news. Respondents cited the abundance of free content available and the belief that publishers already make money from advertising and, therefore, should not require payment directly from the consumer for content (Owens, 2019). In its annual *Digital News Report*, the Reuters Institute for the Study of Journalism reported people would not pay for online news and that there had been only a small increase in the proportion of people willing to do so in the last six years (Faulconbridge, 2019). While the work of many digital Black feminist writers would not readily fit into the traditional news model these studies reference, there is a similar challenge for those who publish their work online. Social media platforms like Twitter made news readily available and free for years before traditional news sites and content creators realized their profit model required paid subscriptions.

While digital Black feminists have begun to monetize online content they had previously offered for free, both Feminista Jones and Luvvie Ajayi also release traditional print books. Ajayi's (2016) *I'm Judging You: The Do-Better Manual* reached the *New York Times* Best Seller list in 2018. Her follow-up *Professional Troublemaker: The Fear-Fighter Manual* (2021) is likewise a best seller. Feminista Jones has written four books, including the 2019 text *Reclaiming Our Space: How Black Feminists Are Changing the World from the Tweets to the Streets*. Both leverage their massive following on Twitter and other social media platforms to increase visibility for print publications. However, high engagement from followers often leads to demands for more labor without payment. In the week of October 14, 2019, Jones received a barrage of tweets demanding that she engage online with a news story about the human trafficking of Black women. Jones, an activist and trained social worker, has supported Black women and girls throughout her career. As she explained, "In case you're wondering, they're talking about Jason Roger Pope, who was arrested for sex trafficking. They're DEMANDING that Blk feminist women tweet about it because apparently, if we don't, we don't care about Blk women. Now you're all smart enough to know why that's corny" (Jones, 2019d). Jones's tweet signals the demands made for instant publication on the terms of her audience. The expectation that digital Black feminists publish their work online for easy access threatens their ability to receive traditional access to publishing that affords compensation.

Anna Julia Cooper's letters to Oberlin, like Jamilah Lemieux's tweets, give insight into both the public and the private world of publishing for Black women thought leaders. Like Cooper, Lemieux insists that her work be treated seriously as a professional writer and scholar. Unlike Cooper, Lemieux has access to a public platform like Twitter. Without restriction or approval, she can respond to the day's events and provide a biting and insightful critique of pop culture and politics. Lemieux could choose to critique publishers and the process openly. She could also avoid traditional publication models, taking advantage of digital options that did not exist for Cooper. However, writing on social media does not bring the same financial security or public recognition of professionalism. An author with a strong social media following is undoubtedly beneficial in the eyes of many print publications, but the expectation that digital Black feminists publish online for free conflicts with the traditional print process. Recognizing this conflict, some writers exit the traditional publishing industry altogether. Others, like Lemieux, fight to carve out space and use digital technology to chart their experiences with publishing. As they press for publication, their online followers must witness their persistence, their success, and their rejections. While Cooper makes this case privately in her letters, digital Black feminist praxis forces a public engagement with the secret world of publishing that makes the gulf between Black feminist thought and industry norms apparent. Lemieux's public discussions about publishing make her audience aware that her online work is the labor of a professional writer. It disabuses them of the notion that she must produce and publish at their request, for free, or when she does not see it as valuable to her career or her cause. Digital Black feminists use their presence on social media to change their relationship with publishing as praxis. That presence also requires digital Black feminists to thread together their lives as private individuals and professional writers.

## Threading and Stitching

In *A Red Record: Tabulated Statistics and Alleged Causes of Lynchings in the United States*, Ida B. Wells-Barnett used data journalism to meticulously document cases of the lynching of Black men and women across the U.S. Wells-Barnett's practice was to document lynching with the belief that she should "tell the world the facts." As she explained, "When the Christian world knows the alarming growth and extent of outlawry in our land, some means will be found to stop it" (Wells-Barnett, 1895, p. 4). Wells-Barnett believed that when all the records were threaded together and the public saw, not individual incidents, but a pattern and practice of lawless violence, action would follow. Wells-Barnett lamented that lynchings only briefly entered the public dialogue, with the topic never being taken seriously enough for a prolonged public interest. As she explained, "No matter how heinous the act of the lynchers may have been, it was discussed only for a day or so and then dismissed from the attention of the public" (Wells-Barnett, 1895, p. 65). Her dogged pursuit of accountability and justice for the countless Black folks murdered in public was an attempt to make the cases amount to more than the sum of their parts. She creates a thread for readers to witness the horror of lynching by seeing it as a persistent, insidious, intentional pattern of terror enacted upon the Black community. Her public work engages the Black feminist praxis of threading, but her private writing provides the mechanism to understanding her intimate relationship with the practice.

### *The Clearing*

Ida B. Wells-Barnett drafted the preface to her autobiography on the back of letters from the Children's Defense Fund and the First Precinct Neighborhood Club of Chicago. In her public writing, Wells-Barnett scratched out, inserted, and stitched ideas together in draft form because, as she concluded, "our youth are entitled to the facts of race history which only the participants can give" (V. P. Franklin, 1995, p. 65). In her private diary, though, she provides a glimpse into the process of becoming a writer and the labor of stitching together her public work and personal life. Literary scholar Mary Helen Washington notes that the most salient theme in the diary is Wells-Barnett's tension between prescribed roles for her as a woman and her passion and drive as a writer. She begins the diary, Washington explains, as a "clearing," a place where the "true self is affirmed." Outside of a physical church house, a clearing, Washington describes, was significant for Black folks and specifically Black women who required a "private sanctuary" to "speak freely" (Wells-Barnett et al., 1995, p. x). In her Memphis diary—her clearing—Wells-Barnett tangles with expectations for Black women, her desire for love, her insecurities about her work, and the passion that propelled her to prominence within the civil rights movement. Her public audience is not privy to this intimate stitching process. Wells-Barnett carefully works through this process in her private writing, disentangling her public image from her private self, a process taken up very differently by digital Black feminist writers online.

Shortly after the television series *Surviving R. Kelly* began airing on Lifetime, Jamilah Lemieux, who was prominently featured in the docuseries and had been calling for accountability for the R&B singer for decades, penned a piece in the *Huffington Post*. In it, she writes,

> We've long understood that the violent, racist nature of law enforcement means that we cannot seek police aid when we are harmed by one of our own men without risking the possibility that he will be harmed by a responding officer. . . . But letting Black men escape accountability isn't some sort of retribution for our ancestors who were murdered over false accusations, or for our peers who languish behind bars for crimes that they did not commit. Those of us who really care about justice should focus on creating a world where the race of an abuser will not protect him from punishment, nor ensure that he will be unduly punished.
>
> We cannot undo the darkness of our past or our present by protecting Black men who abuse Black women under the auspices of "racial solidarity." Furthermore, attempts to let men like Kelly off the hook because of their race implies that Black men are either inherently predisposed to sexual violence or that Black girls and women are inherently incapable of being be victimized. (Lemieux, 2019a, para. 9)

Lemieux and others have spent decades exposing the sexual assault of countless Black girls and women at the hands of R. Kelly.[12] In the article, she recounted her personal experience growing up in Chicago, witnessing, as so many of us did in the 1990s and 2000s, the singer waiting outside of high schools and middle schools to pick up our friends and classmates. Her witness bore space for the clearing provided to survivors in dream hampton's docuseries *Surviving R. Kelly*.[13] Just as Lemieux does in her article, digital Black feminists intentionally stitch together their public and private lives and personas online. In digital forums, Lemieux connects her experiences with the facts of the case. The case against Kelly is stronger for readers *because of* her subjective experience, not despite it. Whereas Wells-Barnett expresses a desire to present the facts, believing her audiences cannot ignore them, Lemieux is certain her audience has willfully ignored the facts for decades as Black women and girls suffered violence at the hands of Kelly. Instead, Lemieux stitches together the pain and anger of racism well understood by the Black community with the shame and silence around violence enacted upon women and girls by Black men. Her argument, her examples, and her writing connect the fate of Black women as survivors of assault and sexual violence with Black men, whom she argues must be on the side of justice even when the perpetrator of these acts is also a Black man. She creates a thread from her own experience to Kelly's victims, and finally, to the readers, she attempts to convince them of his crimes.

I use the words *stitching* and *threading* to consider the piecing together of one's work as a Black feminist writer with one's personal life. Stitching and threading evoke two acts of import for Black women—Twitter threads and the physical threads and stitches used in the process of sewing and quilting. Threading in digital communication is a practice of linking together multiple tweets on the platform of Twitter. Threads often indicate in the first or second tweet that users will be creating a thread. The thread acts as a linkage between related ideas and a means to engage in microblogging on the platform. Rather than being restricted by 140 and later 280 characters, threading, when done well, may link many tweets together to expand an argument and document validation of claims. It also provides a means for the tweeter to link out to the work of others. Perhaps more than any of the other digital Black feminists I encountered while writing this book, Feminista Jones most regularly and successfully uses Twitter to discuss both personal and social justice issues in the same thread. Not relegating this work to a personal diary, her Black feminist praxis requires undertaking this emotional and intellectual work in a digital space that functions as both a private sanctuary and a public forum filled with trolls and hate speech.

Black feminists online are often told to ignore hate speech and online harassment, especially when it comes to Black men. In what began as a discussion of the sexual assault of actor Terry Crews, Jones interjected when a follower suggested she should ignore hate speech from repeat offenders. On January 24, 2019, Jones tweets, "Some of us feel we've been left to fend for ourselves against his [Tariq Nasheed] relentless attacks . . . like ppl simply decide to ignore him and the violence he continued to enact upon BW/queer ppl. IDK if leaving him alone works" (Jones, 2019b). She follows this with an eight-tweet thread where she connects specific incidents of online harassment against herself, Jamilah Lemieux, and Tarana Burke to explain the insidious nature of toxic masculinity. She uses the thread to educate followers about Black men's complicity by ignoring these attacks. She calls her followers to direct action. As she explains, "Some just need to admit they are afraid of him and his influencers and don't want to be harassed the way he and his minions harass us. Just admit you're fine with attacking us and our families and friends as long as it doesn't turn to you" (Jones, 2019b). Jones connects her own life experience and expertise to create a more extended, hyperlinked argument for her followers. Jones threads content about Black women through the lens and expertise of a Black woman but often for an audience who may be hostile toward Black women. Like other digital Black feminists, she threads a metaphorical needle, complicating narratives about Black women, doing Black feminist work in a public space, and stitching together profoundly personal stories with activist work. She uses this public-private space as her clearing. In her book, Jones pens an essay titled "Thread!" in which she explains the importance of this practice online for herself and other Black folks engaged in thought work and public scholarship in this space. She explains, "There is power in the ability to control the narrative in real-time, and Black women have harnessed this power to shut down much of the opposition they face when simply trying to share their experiences as Black women in the world" (Jones, 2019a, p. 45). She engages in this digital Black feminist praxis and theorizes about its origins and capacities for movement building. Her public scholarship traces a history of digital Black feminist praxis and situates it in its rightful place as crucial within the development of a larger American technoculture.

## The Boring Work

Wells-Barnett's practice of stitching in her own life requires an awareness of how others view her and how she feels forced to comport herself as a result. Her diary speaks to her relationship with this practice. Privately, she reveals the pressures of the life of a Black woman activist and writer whose identities are publicly at war with one another. She chooses, "instead of domesticity, an active male-related career while following a Victorian script in her personal life. The tension between these two ways of being is apparent in the diary. She provocatively juxtaposes her private life, her relationships with friends and associates, social and cultural activities, and domestic arrangements against her public life as a teacher and journalist" (Wells-Barnett et al., 1995, p. 4). Publicly, Wells-Barnett was a virulent advocate for antilynching legislation, using her skill and platform as a writer and journalist to document heinous violence and acts of terrorism. When writing for a mass audience, she does not focus on herself. She instead devotes her attention to the cause of racial justice. In her diary, though, she reveals the unease of this relationship to her stitching praxis. Wells-Barnett laments that her motherly instincts may have been destroyed by activism, a deeply personal and painful reckoning (Wells-Barnett et al., 2020). She explores the dichotomies between her professional desires and public personas, making visible the often unsupported and painful praxis of a Black feminist writer. Jones, though, details the power and agency involved in piecing together one's life in public as an act of "sociopolitical analysis, critical gender and race theor[izing], and cultural commentary . . . often developed on the fly, in real-time" (Jones, 2019a, p. 45). In her threads, she engages in a public scholarship, developing a theory or argument as she would in a series of essays or articles while carefully responding to critique and challenge from the audience and reader in real time. For digital Black feminists, threading, as praxis, requires immediate public responsiveness with little time for the kind of private stitching Wells-Barnett does in her diaries. By stitching together their private and public worlds, digital Black feminists capitalize on a long-standing Black feminist praxis, threading.

I also use the word *thread* to remind us of the physical act of "women's work." The activity and techniques of women's work, including Black feminist thought work, are rarely examined apart from what they create. Weaving, sewing, quilting, and knitting, long considered women's work, have historically been techniques considered less than technical. The use of *craft* rather than *art* or *labor* to describe these skills devalues and domesticates the work that often belongs to women. Likewise, because of the importance of their work and the brilliance of their arguments, Wells-Barnett's journalism and Jones's and Lemieux's online writing may lead us to focus on the artifacts they produce. However, like quilting projects that require attention to stitching of material and threading of needles, Black feminist writers threading ideas online are doing the "unsexy, detail-oriented, iterative" (S. Brown, 2018, p. 268) work, which is as important as the artifacts they create. Capturing, publishing, and threading allows us to examine Black feminist praxis before turning to their work product. In other words, studying digital Black feminist praxis focuses on "all those boring things—the meticulous work of moving from a prototype to production, of debugging and updating, the care, repair, and maintenance" (S. Brown, 2018, p. 268) required to move Black feminist thought forward in the digital era. Focus on the process has allowed us to consider the relationships that Black feminists form with digital tools and the principles that guide and are born from their use. Our relationships with technology do not begin with digital technology and anthropomorphized virtual agents like Siri, Alexa, and Google Hubs.[14] As human-machine communication scholars make clear, we have always had relationships with our technologies; the humanoid features of modern tech simply make these relationships more apparent. Black feminist thinkers form relationships with the technologies to do the work of Black feminism on and offline. As Tate (1983) writes about Black women authors, "They project their vision of the world, society, community, family, their lovers, even themselves. . . . Their angle of vision allows them to see what white people, especially white males seldom see. With one penetrating glance they cut through layers of institutionalized racism and sexism and uncover a core of social contradictions and intimate dilemmas which plague all of us, regardless of our race or gender" (p. xvi). They do this while contending with society's capture of their words and their likeness, finding agency in the ability to reorient our gaze and control their own images. Black feminist writers disseminate their words, often fighting against institutions that would relegate their work to the margins. We have now considered the *how* of digital Black feminism by focusing on praxis. In the chapter that follows, I consider the implications of Black feminist thought as a product, moving online, and being born of digital tools and culture.

# 5

## Digital Black Feminism as a Product, or "It's Funny How Money Change a Situation"

In the film *Brown Sugar* (Famuyiwa, 2002), Sidney Shaw, a writer for the hip-hop magazine *XXL*, begins each interview the same way. She asks the artists, "When did you fall in love with Hip-Hop?" *Brown Sugar* is a romantic comedy from the early 2000s featuring a mostly Black cast that traces the history of hip-hop by sketching the extended love affair between two friends who met as children and fall in love as adults. The characters' love lives symbolize the arc of the history of hip-hop. Sidney and Dre find their way back to each other as they find their way back to "real" hip-hop. Thus the film asks us as an audience to consider the origin of the main characters' and our own relationship to hip-hop. As Ravynn Stringfield explains, "The film is comprised of layers upon layers that, like a quilt, like Hip-Hop, when stitched together creates a harmony of narratives read as one. Hip-Hop, like writing, is essential to her [Sydney Shaw] self-making, her self-expression, and her liberation" (Stringfield, 2020). The questions posed by Shaw require people for whom hip-hop is a central part of their lives to reflect on a time when it was not and to try to disentangle themselves from something that feels central to the core of their being. The characters and the audience together interrogate how hip-hop becomes a central part of their careers, personal lives, and culture and does so often without them ever deciding that it would. In her book *She Begat This*, Joan Morgan (2018) similarly asks hip-hop feminists to reflect upon the twentieth anniversary of the album *The Miseducation of Lauryn Hill*, using the album to understand how feminism shifted due to the cultural imprint of Hill and hip-hop culture. In the book, Black women consider their relationship to Hill, a figure and archetype of a specific era of hip-hop where Black women began to see and hear themselves reflected in the music they loved. *Miseducation*, for many of those interviewed, triggered nostalgia for a bygone era in hip-hop.

In the film *Brown Sugar* and reflections from *She Begat This*, characters and writers grapple with hip-hop's current mass appeal and its impact on the genre and the culture. The injection of real money via the record industry in the late 1990s and early 2000s brought hip-hop a new audience and a new sound. Hip-hop went mainstream, with most hip-hop now consumed by non-Black audiences. Morgan's reflections in *She Begat This* and the film *Brown Sugar* ask what happens when hip-hop transitions from being a part of the Black cultural experience to a consumable good for white audiences. When culture is bought and sold, what impact does it have on those who created it? Can it survive? Moreover, what becomes of those who recognize the potential to make money by selling their own culture?

On the first track on Lauryn Hill's *Miseducation*, she raps, "It's funny how money change a situation," before going on to verbally decimate her former bandmate and drop one of the top five diss tracks of all time. Hill comments on how relationships change when money is involved. Complications arise when friends see their goals and practices shift in the wake of their changing relationship to hip-hop as a source of income. Hill's commentary in this track underscores the changing relationship between herself and bandmates and the ever-growing relationship of hip-hop to a mainstream audience and its implications on the authenticity of the art. Hip-hop as a product must be packaged and sold to the widest possible audience. Money changes the situation for Hill and for hip-hop feminists who now must contend with their art being a business. In this chapter, I attempt a similar moment of reflection and pause for digital Black feminism.

Digital Black feminists' relationship with social media is analogous to the relationship hip-hop feminists had to hip-hop. Hip-hop culture was transformative for how many developed and began their relationship with feminism. Then they watched as hip-hop became a commodity, bought and sold by those outside the community. This disconnect is summed up by characters in *Brown Sugar* this way: "Sidney 'Syd' Shaw: [narrating] So, what is the difference between rap and hip-hop? It's simple. It's like the difference between saying you love somebody and being in love with somebody. Rap is just a word." When mainstream America began to consume hip-hop culture as "rap," it became a *thing*. Now profitable, it lost much of what made it transformative and transgressive. Digital Black feminists grew up alongside digital technology the same way hip-hop feminists grew up alongside hip-hop. They began their relationship with social media and digital technology with flip phones and BlackPlanet, long before ad space, influencer culture, Patreon, and paid endorsements. In the early days of Black digital spaces, profitability was less critical than community building and networking. As blogger Luvvie Ajayi explains, "The beauty of blogging, or starting blogging when no one was expecting much from it, is that with that lack of expectation we were able to crack our voices in the exact way we wanted to carve it, and we were able to write as if nobody was reading" (Jun & Ajayi, 2018). However, as Facebook opened up beyond ".edu" email addresses and the *New York Times* began covering Black folks' late-night conversations on Twitter, many digital Black feminists embraced the digital marketplace. In this book, I write about the Black women bloggers who created enclaves online in the early 2000s, developing high-context content for large numbers of loyal followers. Their virtual beauty shops engaged in the kind of branding that advertisers now recognize as profitable. Digital Black feminists maximized platform affordances and paved the way for digital Black feminist content profitable for companies and the Black women that produce it.

In the previous chapters, I argued that the ubiquity of digital culture in digital Black feminists' lives created a fundamental shift in the principles and praxes of Black feminist thought. Like Sidney Shaw, I am now interested in when digital Black feminists fell in love with the digital and how that love affair has affected their relationship to emancipatory Black feminist thought. As we dive headfirst into digital Black feminism, we must consider what has changed about Black women's relationship to Black feminism as seen through their principles and praxes and what it is about the digital that has made space for this shift. While many carry the same liberatory goals as their Black feminist foremothers, digital culture consumes Black feminism as a product. What happens when money changes the situation and Black feminist thought becomes an online product? In this chapter, I outline how Black feminists have mastered the digital age's corporatized and commodified culture. Drawing on examples of Black feminist products distributed across platforms, I demonstrate how Black feminist practices, ideas, and bodies are for sale online. I then offer cautions of how digital Black feminist thought as a product has potentially negative consequences on Black feminism as a liberation model.

## Branding: Ashiness and Shea Butter Twitter

Ashiness provided one of the most GIF-able and meme-able moments of *The Real Housewives of Atlanta*. This is no small feat, as the show, like many reality shows, has produced some of the most GIF-able content on television.[1] On this Bravo television reality show based in Atlanta, Georgia, cast member Porsha Williams walked out of a restaurant with show villain Kenya Moore. As the two traded verbal barbs, Williams waved and said, "Bye, Ashy." Without context, the phrase is insulting, but with context, one realizes the extent of the damage. Humorist and blogger Damon Young writes, "Public Ashiness might be the only thing in the Black community with a 0% approval rating. It's the bane of Black existence; a plague we collectively wish to be eradicated. I'm actually shocked we haven't had any 'End Ash Forever' telethons" (Young, 2016). Dave Chappelle even created a character named Ashy Larry on his hit sketch comedy show *Chapelle's Show*. To be ashy simply means to lack moisture and have skin resembling ash gray in color. Dry skin happens to people of all races; however, dry skin can become more noticeable on people with a darker complexion. Within the Black community, there is an assumption that your parents taught you to moisturize as a child to avoid ashiness. An adult's decision not to moisturize is a decision to present yourself publicly as unkempt and is embarrassing and potentially even shameful.

The denotative meaning is one small part of its use in the Black community. Beyond the dictionary definition, *ashy* is also a word used to describe anything that is just "a bit off." To be ashy is to not care about self-presentation or the expectations of one's community. A person or event can be ashy if they are not quite right in their display, bordering on laughable or disdain inducing. Ashiness is also indicative of those who spurn others in their community, specifically Black men who are hostile to Black women. The multiple meanings of ashy all derive from the denotative meaning, but the connotations are particular to expectations

Figure 5.1. On the left, Porsha Williams yells "Bye, Ashy" to Kenya Moore on *The Real Housewives of Atlanta*. On the right is Ashy Larry, a character from the sketch comedy show *Chappelle's Show*.

within the in-group. The deviation from these expectations allows the word to become a signifier, carrying a broader meaning that requires contextual understanding and in-group status.

## Black Feminist Signifyin'

Signifyin' is a cultural tradition with a long history in the Black community. In Standard American English, the term *signifying* refers to the denotation of meaning through a sign or word. Within the African American community, the term generally refers to a verbal contest where the most imaginative user of indirection, irony, and insult wins (Lee, 1993). It is an elaborate, indirect form of goading or insult, at times making use of profanity (Bell, 1987). Signifyin' is also defined as implying, goading, or boasting by indirect verbal or gestural means (Abrahams, 1999). Lee defines signifyin' as this: "to speak with innuendo and double meanings, to play rhetorically upon the meaning and sounds of words, and to be quick and often witty in one's response" (Lee, 1993, p. 11). The origin of the term *signifyin'* is commonly ascribed to the poem "The Signifying Monkey," a story recounted in music and comedy routines since the beginning of the twentieth century. The Signifying Monkey is a character of African American folklore that derives from Esu Elegbara, the trickster figure of Yoruba mythology (Gates, 2014). In this poem, set in the jungle, a monkey repeatedly hurls insults at a lion, claiming that he is merely repeating an elephant's words. As the lion becomes increasingly enraged, he decides to confront the elephant. The elephant beats the lion mercilessly. The lion realizes that the monkey has tricked him and has only been "signifyin."

According to Gates, signifyin' "functions as a metaphor for formal revision, or intertextuality, within the Afro-American literary tradition" (Gates, 2014, p. xxii). In this context, authors reuse motifs from previous works, altering them and "signifying" upon them to create their own meanings. Gates suggests that the verbal wordplay of African Americans is spiritual and jovial, connecting Black Americans to West African traditions while employing the cunning necessary to evade detection within the context of a hateful and violent chattel slavery system. As Levine explains, "The need to laugh at our enemies, our situation, ourselves is a common one, but exists more urgently in those who exert the least power over their immediate environment" (Levine, 2007, p. 300). Signifyin' as a form of oratorical wordplay and humor is used to critique the community's negative characteristics as a form of community self-disciplining. A white person's skin can lack moisture, but as pejorative, ashy works best when levied between two Black people because the expectation is that *they* should not be ashy. If that expectation does not carry for other groups, they cannot be signified upon in this way. To be called ashy as a Black person is to be disciplined for failing to do what one should do, either (1) apply lotion (if being literal) or (2) be supportive of other Black people—namely, women (if used to signify).

On Twitter, the term *ashy* is used in conjunction with the term *Hotep* to describe a form of Black masculinity that is hostile to Black women and femmes. While possessing a separate denotative meaning, in progressive Black circles, *Hotep* critiques a form of Blackness that appears to embrace Black people but traffics in politics that are misogynistic, antiprogressive, and conspicuously Afrocentric. Ashy, when used pejoratively online, signals that one's point of view, as expressed in a tweet or post, is indicative of adherence to an ideology of Black empowerment that ignores Black women or the Black community. Ashiness is showing no commitment to ensuring *all* Black folks get free. In Damon Young's (2018a) article "The 10 Ashiest People in America, Ranked," he says this of Clarence Thomas (who ranks at number ten): "Conservative politics and perpetually chapped lips are a clear sign of lotion avoidance." He goes on to describe Dr. Boyce Watkins, saying, "The sheer and luminous ash of Dr. Watkins blaming our wealth and education disparities on . . . *Black women buying weave* (???) must be acknowledged and praised for its ashy integrity. He is truly committed to dust." These two Black men hold opposing political beliefs, with Thomas openly distancing himself from policies that would benefit Black Americans and Watkins claiming to be an advocate for Black empowerment. Yet Young marks both as ashy for using their platform in ways that place them at odds with freedom and justice for *all* Black Americans. Black men that willfully ignore or openly condemn Black women are ashy. They both are worthy candidates to be signified upon by digital Black feminists. Like many other Black oratorical practices, Black men have often been the focus of study for signifying and dozens play. Overlooked are Black women's signifying practices often used as mechanisms of critique against Black men.

## From Identity to Brand Management

Lee proposes that signifyin' is a "powerful intellectual tool that goes unnoticed, devalued, and untapped. Signifyin' is not merely a discursive artifact, but also serves as a medium for the internal organization of experience and a heuristic for problem-solving that requires analogical reasoning" (Lee, 1993, p. 22). Zora Neale Hurston describes signifyin' as "big picture talk[ing] . . . using a side of the world for a canvas" (Hurston, 2006, p. 51). The ability to participate expertly in signifyin' requires the signifier to understand the scope and breadth of the world in which they live and position themselves and those whom they signify upon within it. Digital Black feminists use platforms like Twitter to course correct within the community and resist external classification by others. They use signifyin' as a discursive tool to organize people and participate in a project of identity negotiation. For Black feminists, signifyin' is "empowering and potentially culturally self-defining" (Lee, 1993, p. 16). The deployment of signifyin' to joke, resist, and relish in the libidinal existed far before Black Twitter.[2] However, in socially mediated spaces, the need to identify and present a coherent self to the public becomes even more pronounced. Social media platforms require this type of engagement for participation. Black feminists use signifyin' online to resist external classification, produce culturally specific dialogue and discourse, inscribe new modes of categorization and organization, and ultimately create and forge their own identities.

While identity and branding are separate enterprises, for many Black feminists online, the management of each comes from a skill honed by the same set of experiences. Labels like "Ashy Twitter" and "Hotep Twitter" come in part from Black feminists who are calling out Black men for their shortcomings as advocates for Black women and gender non-binary folks. Likewise, "Pick-Me Twitter" developed as a label for other Black women who use their platforms to espouse patriarchal beliefs or prop up men who do. This labeling is more than name-calling or jovial dozens play. Black feminists use signification to be explicit about their own identities and their online brands. Digital Black feminists rely on agency and the dialectic of self and community interests to connect identity negotiation to branding as a means for self-empowerment and a potential revenue stream. Creating a brand online requires digital Black feminists to use skill sets that were already required offline to engage with a broader audience and turn that engagement into profit.

Ashy men are a visible and useful foil that helps create a brand for digital Black feminism. In response to being called "ashy" online, some men have begun using "Shea-butter Twitter" pejoratively to describe Black feminists online. Rather than insulting, this label is brand reinforcing. If Black feminists call out Black men's malfeasance by branding them as ashy, signifying upon the signifiers as moisturized gravely misses the mark. Culturally and contextually, moisture is appropriate, and ashiness is not. Callouts like these are both an act of community regulation and critique and a useful technique of self-promotion. Digital Black feminists do not separate these two needs. Therefore, signifying demonstrates the power of branding as an exercise of digital Black feminism and the effectiveness of this tool when used correctly.

## The Conflation of Self-Naming and Branding

In her transformative text *When and Where I Enter*, Paula Giddings (1984) describes Black women activists' work as a defense of their names, which have been and continue to be tarnished as a means to deprive them of their full rights as citizens. In antilynching movements, women's clubs, and speeches for voting rights, "naming" is an agentic practice. Black women—too frequently called out of their names—use their rhetorical skills to name themselves, rename, and rebrand others. In her memoir *Eloquent Rage*, Black feminist writer and scholar Brittney Cooper described coming to her self-naming after a childhood wherein she was othered. She explains, "So much of what it meant to be a Black girl among white girls, was to be a spectator and coconspirator in their construction of me as the other" (B. C. Cooper, 2018, p. 50). Anna Julia Cooper suggests that the confining role of Black womanhood often keeps *naming* from Black women's reach. Black women face subordination from white folks but are also "hampered and shamed by a less liberal sentiment and a more conservative attitude on the part of those for whose opinion she cares most" (A. J. Cooper, 2017, p. 573). Dual subordination based on both race and gender prohibits full access to the process of self-naming for Black women. However, the digital environment provides an opportunity to resist external naming structures and controlling images of Black women. Socially mediated environments require acts of naming for participation. Online, the path from naming as a liberatory practice to branding as a financial necessity for Black women is a relatively short walk.

The conflation of self-naming practices and branding is a hallmark of digital Black feminism. Digital Black feminists use Twitter, Facebook, and the blogosphere, which provided free space for content creators to craft brand images. Initially, corporations benefited from this work through the ad revenue generated through the user's content creation. However, as their brands grew, many developed revenue streams based on the brands they created there. Luvvie Ajayi has created her own social networking platform using the Mighty Networks.[3] There she directs users to her podcast, paid events, books, and other online writing. Feminista Jones, who has been a prolific user of Twitter over the years, amassing more than 150,000 followers, left the platform briefly in 2019, pushing her content to Patreon. Though back on Twitter in 2020, Jones's followers access videos and long-form writing via her Patreon page via a paid monthly subscription. Jones also released her fourth book in 2019. Mikki Kendall, who also has built a large following on Twitter and is the creator of the #SolidarityIsForWhiteWomen hashtag, publishes short stories and essays on Patreon. Her book *Hood Feminism* was released in 2020. Each has built a brand online based in part on their image as a Black feminist writer. Each has now monetized this brand successfully using platform and content distribution innovations.

These Black feminist writers have successfully translated their success on social media to other arenas wherein they might benefit financially and professionally. Online stores and service-based businesses are a couple means by which Black feminist deploy their branding skill set. Black feminists are also branding Black feminism for consumption. However, bell hooks (2000b) reminds us of the danger of feminism itself becoming a brand. As a facet of identity or part of a brand, hooks suggests that Black feminism moves away from the revolutionary struggle. She critiques branded feminism as performative and restrictive in that labels can confine via expectations and stereotypes. hooks pushes for a focus on the work of Black feminism rather than the label shifting from "I am a feminist" to "I advocate for feminism" (hooks, 2000b). While digital Black feminists also resist labels from the outside, they reclaim self-branding as an agentic practice. They create the lens through which others will see them and use that lens to sell products and create a reliable network of followers. Digital Black feminists are naming themselves through their brand and relying on Black oral traditions like signifyin' to deploy a Black feminist brand online intentionally.

Utilizing Black rhetorical strategies and Black feminist resistance frameworks in pursuit of branding does raise questions for many about the revolutionary potential of digital Black feminism in the long term. While Black feminists, as a part of their brand strategy, name and define themselves and others, this is not always synonymous with naming oppression. Put forward in the Combahee River Collective statement on Black feminism, the authors suggest, "We realize the liberation of all oppressed people necessitates the destruction of the political-economic systems of capitalism and imperialism as well as patriarchy. We are socialists because we believe that the work must be organized for the collective benefit of those who do the work and create the products, and not for the profit of the bosses" (Combahee River Collective, 1983, p. 274). Digital platforms provide a gray area of labor and profit. Black feminists contend with a digital marketplace that allows for individual agency and profit while being tied to corporatized structures that reproduce uneven power differentials. Digital Black feminists refuse to choose between branding and revolution, deploying their branded images to pursue their businesses and in the service of others. They disrupt the bifurcation of workers and bosses as they turn their digital platforms and their brands as Black feminists into commercial enterprises. Branding provides one avenue to understand digital Black feminism as a product. Beyond the branding of individuals, digital technologies are also packaging Black feminist theory for sale.

## Selling the Goods: Intersectional Pizza and Self-Care Checklists

### Black Feminist Buzzwords

Akilah Hughes (2015), a writer and comedienne, created a YouTube video in 2015 that explained the premise of intersectionality using the metaphor of pizza. Hughes described men as burgers and women as pizza, with cheese pizza as the stand-in for white women and deluxe pizza as the stand-in for Black women. She described Black women's exclusion from mainstream white feminist causes and the additional burden Black women face as they advocate for their freedom. She did so by lightheartedly discussing pizza toppings. The video went viral and was reposted on many blogs and even shared on cable news networks. Hughes, it seemed, was onto something. The short video was packaged in a way that held the attention of a public increasingly used to consuming content in short, digestible bites. It took material usually considered challenging and made it easy to understand, and it did so without alienating any viewers. Americans love pizza and burgers, and pizza and burgers, unlike the people they are meant to represent, do not hold any responsibility for how their existence impacts the existence of others.

As a teacher, especially one who teaches about white supremacy and patriarchy with the belief that Black feminist thought is revolutionary, I have spent years practicing the art of introducing both resistant and open-minded students to these ideas in the classroom. Being a teacher is, in many ways, like being a salesperson. Teaching white folks about white supremacy and men about patriarchy is akin to being a telemarketer or door-to-door salesperson calling on a client at dinnertime. Your product may be excellent, but your presence is rarely welcome. Likewise, there is never a good time to tell someone that they benefit from a system of power, and the means to a more equitable society is through them relinquishing power they may not have even known that they had. So when digital videos and hashtags emerge that package complex theory into bite-sized chunks that students will pay attention to, it is tempting to embrace and even encourage their use. Intersectionality pizza may provide an attractive metaphor for students, but buzzwords and viral videos do not provide the tools for in-depth critical analysis.

As a medium of mass communication, digital platforms can package the ideas of Black feminism for sale. However, the commodification process provides superficial access to complex theories culminating in a more watered-down product palatable to a broader audience. Intersectionality and the matrix of domination are complex theoretical frameworks. As an instructor, I would introduce students to more advanced material only after they demonstrate their ability to comprehend and apply introductory ideas. Online, though, users are provided quick and easy access to theory before doing the work of self-examination and critical reflection. When presented with simple ways of understanding complex experiences and theory, viewers bank knowledge rather than engaging in analysis. Paulo Freire (1970/2006) argues that formal education compels students to "bank" knowledge to dispense it later for reward, often via test taking. This kind of instruction leaves no space for critical analysis. Instead, students simply regurgitate banked knowledge during prescribed scenarios. Outside the classroom, we continue to "bank" knowledge through the fast-paced world of twenty-four-hour cable news and in the manageable chunks of 140 or 280 characters on Twitter. In each environment, we store up bits of information that we may recall later. However, we tend to recall it only in the form first provided because the sheer amount of information passed along prevents careful interrogation. Intersectionality as pizza may be a useful tool for reinforcing a concept, but it is not as useful in teaching the public a complex theoretical argument about power and domination. For those already familiar with intersectionality, the metaphor is fun and engaging. However, as a first introduction, it is insufficient and better suited as bankable content than a road map for serious analysis.

Online content that produces high arousal, whether positive or negative, is more likely to go viral than that which evokes "low activating" emotion or requires sustained analysis. Content that immediately evokes joy or anger is more profitable than that which produces feelings of confusion, despair, or sadness (Berger & Milkman, 2012). Making clickable and shareable products results in more engagement for advertisers.[4] Creating content or sharing the high-engagement content of others provides a substantial reward. It is incredibly challenging to package nuanced and contextually rich content into a short video and produce immediate high arousal. Clickable viral content cannot afford to waste time describing how burgers (men) created and reinforce a system that makes cheese pizza (white women) and deluxe pizza (Black women) inferior. Nor can it explain how cheese pizzas (white women) are complicit in the oppression of deluxe pizzas (Black women). Intersectionality pizza has a high arousal factor, primarily because it requires little sustained or critical analysis. The metaphor used in the video relies on gender binaries, is devoid of context and critiques about power, and instead provides a metaphor that mostly resonates with those already familiar with concepts like privilege. Too much complexity or nuance would make viewers unable to respond immediately with high arousal (either positive or negative). Discussing white women's complicity in white supremacy or how Black men benefit from patriarchy requires more time and lower arousal from the audience. In this way, concepts like intersectionality lose much of their rich legacy when they *go viral*.

## Undoing the Damage

Clickable and hashtaggable Black feminism may circulate quickly but produces unintended consequences. Ayesha Curry is a businesswoman, a public personality, and the wife of NBA star Stephen Curry. Curry has increased attention on her family based on her husband's meteoric rise in the NBA and has successfully launched multiple businesses predicated on her household and culinary skills. Without their consent but perhaps with their tacit approval, the Currys became a modern stand-in for acceptable and respectable Blackness. They were a young religious family with fame and fortune but without any controversy. In 2015, though, Ayesha waded into the waters of respectability more deeply by tweeting, "Everyone's into barely wearing clothes these days huh? Not my style. I like to keep the good stuff covered up for the one who matters" (Curry, 2015). Many argued that Curry was using her "wholesome" image to devalue other women, reinforcing tropes that are all too common regarding Black women's worthiness and respectability. In the years that followed, some never forgave Curry's comments. As Jamilah Lemieux tweeted, "Four years ago, she made a comment about modest clothing and folks have acted like she's the president of the Mean Girls Patriarchy Fan Club ever since. Y'all forgot about the part where feminism gives us freedom to choose how we move in the world, eh?" (Lemieux, 2019c). Lemieux's tweet came as Curry sat down with Jada Pinkett Smith for her web series *Red Table Talk* to discuss her life as a young mom and wife to an NBA superstar. On the show, she admitted to feeling insecure about her body after having children. Curry explained how demoralizing it is to watch your partner receive attention while struggling with feelings of self-worth and value, especially after your body has changed so much. In the same interview, she discussed her journey with anxiety and the medication she takes to live with the disorder. Reaction on Twitter was swift and harsh.

The critique Curry received came from two seemingly different groups. The first was "ashy men" and "pick-me women," both judging Curry's insecurities and suggesting her candid discussion was embarrassing and disrespectful to her husband. Separately, Curry was shown little sympathy by some claiming to be feminists. They suggested her insecurities and low self-esteem resulted from her acceptance of patriarchal culture, respectability, and misogynistic views on marriage.

Black feminist buzzwords like *misogynoir, intersectionality*, and *respectability* were levied at Curry to shame and undermine her expression of anxiety and insecurity. However, digital Black feminist principles act as a shield from the barrage of criticism. Many writers like Jamilah Lemieux and Kimberly Nicole Foster pushed for introspection. Foster, the creator of *For Harriet*, a blog written by and for Black women, first responded on Twitter. She pushed back against the critique of Curry, noting, "Ayesha is not the problem. She is the victim of the same shit the rest of us are dealing with. She's just unlucky enough to do it as a public figure. To make fun of that and bring up her use of medication is UGLY. Idk [I don't know] what feminist texts y'all follow, but reread them" (Foster, 2019). Foster and Lemieux provide a realignment to a misinterpretation and misapplication of Black feminist thought. After expressing her discontent with what she saw as a superficial treatment of Black feminist thought, Foster shifted to a platform that allowed for deeper engagement. *For Harriet*, Foster's blog, rarely produces long-form written content anymore. Like many digital Black feminist bloggers, Foster has moved on from blogging to produce other digital content like YouTube videos and vlogs that are more accessible and shareable. On her vlog, she crafts a sustained argument for viewers who may have had little understanding of Black feminist thought before viewing. She explained ideas like respectability and intersectionality in detail and offered additional resources for viewers. Foster chose a platform more appropriate to engage with ideas in complex ways—something tweets and viral content may not allow. A commodified Black feminism requires Black feminists to package thought for sale with clickable content and hashtags. However, digital Black feminists like Foster who have spent a career crafting and honing rhetorical arguments for Black feminism in digital spaces signify their expertise by redistributing Black feminist thought in new digital environments without losing the substance. As Black feminism is increasingly packaged for sale, terms like *intersectionality* and *self-care* become buzzwords and fodder for BuzzFeed woke-ability checklists.[5] Foster, therefore, redirects digital Black feminist discourse to spaces that are still profitable but have the affordances necessary to do more than teach surface-level analysis.

**Jamilah** ✔
@JamilahLemieux

I know why Ayesha Curry makes some women uncomfortable. She represents everything they were told they should be, from her look to her her marital status and role we assume she plays at home. However, there is no excuse for holding her accountable for what society did to you.

11:30 AM · May 7, 2019 · Twitter for iPhone

Figure 5.2. Jamilah Lemieux responds to criticisms of Ayesha Curry. Tweet by @JamilahLemieux, May 19, 2019. Screenshot by author.

*Tweeting to Transgress*

Black feminist thinkers frequently challenge a version of feminism that does not consider the consequences of hypercapitalism and imperialism. Simultaneously, they remind readers that Black women are ignored as intellectuals and experts deserving compensation for their work. As journalism and social media professor of communication Meredith Clark explains,

> Earning wages for my intellectual labor is a fair and just practice; it is a normalized practice in this capitalistic, white hetero-patriarchal social system. . . . I am a Black woman who made a career choice to earn my living as an intellectual. It comes at a steep cost, both socially and economically. Remember the wage gap? The wealth gap? The health disparities reported as statistics, separated from the narratives of the individual and community's lived experiences? Yeah, that's me.
>
> That is what I bring, along with perspective that someone might seek, when I show up to answer questions and provide context about social phenomena. Every dollar I ask for addresses a part of my lived experience—not just the part that is valuable or interesting to you. (Clark, 2020)

While this would seem a contradiction for many, Clark asserts that Black women's labor cannot and should not be free within a capitalistic system. She and other Black feminist thinkers do so even as they fight to dismantle the system itself. When Feminista Jones briefly departed Twitter in 2019, she created a Patreon account wherein users who found her content useful could pay to receive more of it. Her content is deeply transgressive to the boundaries erected by patriarchy, white supremacy, respectability, and Judeo-Christian religiosity—and yet she makes money from its creation. Jones pursues the work of teaching to transgress while operating within a capitalistic system and digital model of content distribution.

In *Teaching to Transgress*, bell hooks (1994) argues that education should provide the "gift of freedom." In her estimation, transgressive teaching practices push against the racial, sexual, and class boundaries that make up traditional education. Barbara Omolade explains that

Black feminist pedagogy does three things: unsettle the power dynamics of the classroom/space, produce interventions in modes of communication, and produce a space where teachers struggle alongside their students for a better university or institution/organization (Omolade, 1987). Moving away from checklists, buzzwords, and bankable knowledge, digital Black feminists like Feminista Jones and Kimberly Nicole Foster employ a radical Black feminist pedagogy in their online work. Knowledge constructed outside of traditional means has the power to be subversive both through content and through the mode of delivery. While grappling with the unintended consequences of Black feminist thought's commodification, digital Black feminist work transgresses white Western models of expertise and knowledge dissemination. Blogs, vlogs, and even Twitter threads allow users to create and disseminate ideas to a willing and engaged group of followers. Socially mediated discussions outside a traditional classroom reside alongside formal writing as acceptable modes of knowledge production. Black feminists construct knowledge using both theory and experience, and this process "decidedly involves the inclusion of the ideas, theories, orientations, experiences, and world views of persons and groups that have been previously excluded" (Thomas, 1998, p. 496). Digital Black feminists turn vlogs and Twitter threads into generative spaces of discourse that dismantle the elitist power dynamics involved in Western teaching.

Black women are beginning to receive notoriety online for their thought work, but Black feminism as a commodity has limits. Intersectional pizza does not provide the substantive tools to dismantle systems of white supremacy and patriarchy. Selling Black feminism raises concerns about whether Black feminists can sustain their relationship with capitalism and profitability online while pushing for systemic change. However, it also reminds us that Black feminists are already managing to do so. As Maria del Guadalupe Davidson (2019) concludes in *Black Women, Agency, and the New Black Feminism*, we can critique a generation of feminists for their perceived shortcomings or listen and learn how their experiences led them to make revisions to Black feminist thought. Disregarding this work as incompatible with Black feminist thought misses how digital culture and digital tools have motivated this shift and what this might mean for the future. Digital tools can help provide new avenues to teach a broader public about

Black feminist thought and praxis. Relying on signifying practices and using viral imagery in the form of GIFs and memes, digital Black feminists have adopted many facets of digital culture while requiring readers and viewers to do more than apply buzzwords to the news of the day. Digital Black feminists operate their virtual beauty shops for profit while using their digital classrooms to teach transgressively. The relationship between digital Black feminism and profit is complicated. This is especially true as we consider how others consume Black women's bodies in a culture of digital profitability.

## Prototypes for Sale: Appropriation, Respectability, and Performativity

### Eating the Other

In 2014, fashion magazine *Marie Claire* tweeted a picture of model Kendall Jenner with the caption "Kendall Jenner takes bold braids to a new epic level" (*Marie Claire*, 2014). When Kylie Jenner posted a picture of herself with cornrows in 2015, actress Amandla Stenberg commented, "When you appropriate Black features and culture but fail to use your position of power to help Black Americans by directing attention towards your wigs instead of police brutality or racism" (Stenberg, 2015). Black women have had years of experience calling out cultural appropriation on social media. They highlight how mainstream white culture has popularized Black women's hair, bodies, and ways of speaking while leaving Black women without support or aid. Like *intersectionality*, *cultural appropriation* has become such a trendy phrase that it has lost meaning for many. However, the Kardashians seem invested in ensuring that the term remains relevant far into the twenty-first century. A media, beauty, and fashion empire propped up by white women's flirtation with Black culture, Black men, and Black aesthetics, the Kardashians have used the appropriation of Black women to build a massive following.

Because the term *appropriation* has become another overused and understudied idea from Black feminist thought, I turn to bell hooks's "eating the other" to describe the damage done to marginalized communities by the scraping of culture for profit. The act of eating the other, described by hooks (1992) in her essay "Eating the Other: Desire and Resistance," explains the dominant group's tendency to use pieces of

**amandlastenberg** left a comment on **kyliejenner**'s photo: @novemberskyys when u appropriate black features and culture but fail to use ur position of power to help black Americans by directing attention towards ur wigs instead of police brutality or racism #whitegirlsdoitbetter

Figure 5.3. "Appropriation" Instagram comment by @amandlastenberg, July 12, 2015. Screenshot by author.

marginalized culture for their gain and to the detriment of the marginal culture. hooks takes the phrase from British slang, where getting "a bit of the other" is a colloquialism for the sexual encounters of white upper-class/middle-class men with "exotic" nonwhite others. Beyond mere cultural appropriation, hooks's essay and her use of this colloquialism remind us of the harm in seeing another human as something to be consumed. hooks paints a vivid metaphor of "eating the other" as cannibalism. She suggests that appropriating is an act of violence enacted upon marginalized communities by dominant groups who wish to metaphorically "eat" them to appear and feel more alive. To appropriate someone's culture is to place oneself in a position of power to determine how, to what extent, and in what spaces the culture is useful and acceptable and in which spaces it is disdainful. This distinction separates appropriation from appreciation. Pain is inflicted on the group when their culture is taken, used, and disregarded when no longer in fashion. "Eating the other" is a violent act that leaves the victim less whole. Black women earn less, are incarcerated more, and are recipients of more state violence than their white counterparts. This is due, in part, to a disregard for Black women's pain and humanity that began in chattel slavery and continues today through the violence of consuming Blackness as a product.

Increasingly stark class distinctions in the Black community make appropriation an in-group threat as well. Poor and working class Black women's culture and aesthetics are in the most danger of appropriation, as they are ripe for adoption by both white folks and upper-middle-class and middle-class Black folks. With increased educational opportunities and economic mobility, many Black Americans find themselves not only working in a predominantly white world but residing in one as well.[6] Those born into working-class and poor Black households are painfully aware of the legacy of oppression in America yet now find themselves in a privileged position within the community. As Lacy suggests, "Blacks who have access to white neighbourhoods and predominantly white work spaces demonstrate concerns about maintaining black social ties and culture" (Lacy, 2004, p. 925). The acquisition of education and financial status creates a struggle to adhere to community centeredness amid a push toward assimilation to middle-class whiteness. Black folks who have by virtue of education maneuvered from working-class roots to a middle-class lifestyle may have to intentionally work at remaining attached to the visible facets of Black culture that were once their own. Events like "trap house brunch parties" and "trap yoga" signal a desire to remain connected to Blackness, but these events use a particular raced and classed Black aesthetic to signal distance from white middle-classness. hooks explains that eating the other is a response to a feeling of emptiness, that being devoid of deep cultural affinity makes one long for an exotic other to feel alive. By this same extension, some within the Black community utilize digital culture and social media to be in proximity to and partake in facets of Black culture as a strategy of resisting assimilation into whiteness. Where is the distinction between affiliation and consumption? Can Black folks eat the other when the other consists of other Black folks? How does our exploration of self and identity online intersect with using others as commodified and consumable objects?

## You Are the Prototype

For Black women of a certain age, it is difficult to consume popular culture without consuming Beyoncé. Syllabi,[7] special issues in journals, and entire academic monographs have been devoted to the importance of Beyoncé as a cultural icon and figure of Black feminist praise and critique. Scholars have delved into her lyrics to discuss Black love relationships, mental health, motherhood, and loss. Pop culture writers have considered Beyoncé's relationship to Black music and Black people through her philanthropy and social justice. In this book, I wrote about Beyoncé as a symbol of both sexual agency and capitalist enterprise. Beyoncé began her career with a wholesome public image, shying away from discussions about her personal life. Later, she used the speculations about her romantic partnerships to fuel interest in her albums and concerts, only making her relationship with Sean Carter (Jay-Z) public in 2004 as the two walked the red carpet together for the first time. Shortly after their wedding in 2008, she branded her concert tour the Mrs. Carter Show, and she slowly began providing images from her child's birth and family life in concert promos, in music videos, and on social media. Finally, the release of *Lemonade* and subsequently *4:44*[8] provided an eager public an even more personal glimpse into the star's relationship. Her public performance of motherhood and marriage happened alongside a more recent foray into sexual exhibition. Yet as many scholars point out, her sexual agency only happens when she becomes a wife and mother. For her most eager fans, Beyoncé serves as an aspirational model. However, her "queen" status among the Beyhive makes her an unrelatable, albeit beloved, figure.[9] Consuming Beyoncé happens from afar, with the star careful of how close she allows fans to her personal life. Unlike Beyoncé, rapper Cardi B serves as a *prototype* for digital Black feminism.

Uncomfortable affiliating with a class and social status that separates them from their communities, some digital Black feminists work through this double consciousness by adopting aesthetics and cultural and linguistic practices of other Black women. Rapper and reality star Cardi B's public performance of sexual and financial agency serves as a test of their desire to be more sexual, more uninhibited, more engaged with their Blackness, and less bound to respectability. Unlike Beyoncé, Cardi B has been less filtered in interviews and social media. Her career and personal life have always been in front of the camera, making more of her image immediately accessible to fans. She first gained acclaim through the reality television series *Love & Hip Hop* but went on to release an album, win a Grammy, and become a hip-hop and social media sensation.[10] Cardi B has openly discussed her past as a stripper and has described her plastic surgeries publicly. She used her previous career as a dancer to fund and create a brand for herself online. While Beyoncé has more recently used speculation about her marriage to fuel album sales, Cardi B's romantic relationships and breakups were public, with the star openly discussing cheating claims about her husband on Instagram Live.[11] She has never proclaimed the mantle of being a Black feminist, yet her career and image, for some, signifies a manifestation of assertions about the primacy of agency in a new digital Black feminism. Combining financial and sexual agency in her breakout song "Bodak Yellow," Cardi B raps,

> My pussy glitter as gold
> Tell that lil' bitch play her role
> I just arrove in a Rolls
> I just came up in a Wraith
> I need to fill up the tank
> No, I need to fill up the safe

Digital Black feminists, whose education or career may separate them physically from Black culture, are eager to make clear their distinction from their white peers. The adoption of a prototype like Cardi B allows them to commodify other Black women's experiences and persona for their benefit. Within a world of trap brunches and ratchet yoga, they perform a version of Blackness absent from their work and home lives. Rapping along to "Money Bag" or "Bickenhead," digital Black feminists utilize other Black women as prototypes to project their image of a ratchet feminist practice.

Black women online are interrogating a contemporary performance of Black feminism that is no longer bound by respectability. Instead, this digital Black feminism is rooted in agency and a dialectic of self and community interests and bound by a digital culture of consumption and commerce. Prototyping allows digital Black feminists to test out some parts of their Black feminist practice. In information science, engineering, and digital humanities, prototyping is essential in the design process. Rikke Dam and Teo Siang (2019), writing for the Interaction Design Foundation, define prototyping as "producing an early, inexpensive, and scaled down version of the product in order to reveal any problems with the current design. Prototyping offers designers the opportunity to bring their ideas to life, to test the practicability of the current design, and to potentially investigate how a sample of users think and feel about a product." While never claiming the mantle of "Black feminist," Cardi B's online image has been treated as a test case for digital Black feminists to try on components of her image for their use. On an Instagram video posted by Cardi B, shared in a public Facebook group, one user wrote the caption "one of the best *uses* of Cardi B I've seen thus far" (emphasis mine; One of the best uses, 2017). Users try on her image, her words, and her dances as they decide the extent of her utility in forming a new image of themselves. Cardi B is Belcalis Almánzaris, a person with goals and desires whose life does not belong to anyone. Her fans did not create her, but in a digital culture where celebrities must package their image, fans treat her as a product for sale. Her public image is an amalgamation of the desires and needs of those who follow her. But using Cardi B in this way creates a box within which she is "useful." Deviating from that box provokes a strong reaction among fans. In September of 2017, Cardi B tweeted, "Bill Clinton got impeached for getting his dick sucked & this [carrot emoji] still president ruining the country in less than a year [confused emoji] [hand on head emoji]" (Almánzaris, 2017). Many responses either shamed or paternalized the rapper. Some wrongly asserted that Bill Clinton was not impeached and mocked Cardi B for getting this detail incorrect.[12] Others asked that

**iamcardib** ✅                                                 ooo
@iamcardib

**Bill Clinton got impeached for getting his dick sucked & this 🥕 still president ruining the country in less than a year 😕 🤦**

8:07 AM · Sep 28, 2017 · Twitter for iPhone

**79.5K** Retweets   **2.6K** Quote Tweets   **206.3K** Likes

Figure 5.4. "Bill Clinton" tweet by @iamcardib, September 28, 2017. Screenshot by author.

fans not mock her but instead extend grace, as she must not have a good grasp of U.S. history. A few months later, when the rapper sat down for an interview with *GQ*, she unleashed her vast knowledge of presidential history. In the 2020 election, Cardi B interviewed Democratic nominees for president.

Nevertheless, some fans continue to treat Cardi B as an intellectual inferior, only useful insomuch as her ratchet public performance inhabits the freedom others wish to possess. Black celebrities are frequently asked to stay out of politics, considered inept and ill-prepared to participate (even as the U.S. elected a white reality star as the forty-fifth president). Therefore, Cardi B is considered useful only when she embodies "ratchet" digital Black feminist practice. Writing for Bitch Media, Raquel Savage explains, "Part of feeling liberated as a woman absolutely can (and does) include moving away from purity politics, (re)learning how to set (monetary) boundaries and expectations of our partners and understanding that autonomy means, 'I own my body, not you.' But it becomes clear that praxis is only allotted to certain people; that dabbling in sexual liberation is for folks who aren't actually hoes, don't actually sell nudes online and don't actually sell pussy" (Savage, 2019). Savage, a sex coach and educator, explains that obsession with "hoe" aesthetics without a commitment to actual sex workers is deeply problematic. In this way, prototyping digital Black feminism online commodifies other Black women, treating people as products who can be replaced and discarded when no longer useful. In a digital age, celebrities acquire, maintain, and cultivate fame based on their ability to successfully utilize online communication technology. Both Beyoncé and Cardi B built brands and used social media to enhance their fame and image. Beyoncé's carefully managed social media accounts reveal intentional, curated glimpses into her life to support a brand she built mostly offline. For Cardi B, though, digital branding through social media catapulted her to fame. As a result, she is treated as a digital object, memed, quoted, and deployed as a prototype during the design process of digital Black feminist thought.

Prototyping as a model for understanding digital Black feminists' relationship to Cardi B is useful because it allows us to consider the process of *constructing* digital Black feminism. Prototyping signals how digitality changes Black feminist thought in both useful and problematic ways. At its best, digital Black feminism is uniquely positioned to bring together voices across class and educational lines to imagine a Black feminist future collaboratively. Black women contribute intellectually to Black feminist thought, regardless of their class status or profession. Outside the academy, Black women challenge elitism, push forward new theory, and design Black feminist praxis online. They are knowledgeable and willful agents in making changes to the extensions and possibilities of Black feminism, not technophobes confined by technologies they do not understand. Focusing on the process is a useful reminder that digital Black feminism is a design endeavor by product developers, and there is labor and intentionality in creating Black feminist thought. However, prototyping also reminds us how bound up digital Black feminism is with capitalism. Digital Black feminists consider a (re)construction of Black feminist principles and praxes using digital technology. They function as engineers making choices about Black feminism as a *product* for sale that must meet the consumer's needs. Digital Black feminists prototype as part of a design process that includes defining a problem, ideating a solution, and eventually testing those solutions for consumers (Dam & Siang, 2019). Breaking the bounds of respectability and embracing one's sexuality through prototyping allow the freedom to *try on* digital Black feminism through online practice. However, a Black feminist practice that prototypes of Black femininity but does so without treating Black women as fully human signifies a threat to the kind of collaborative practice necessary to create a radical and freeing form of Black feminist thought.

Digital Black feminists are technophiles. This is the first generation of Black women to use digital technology to find romantic and sexual partners, draft presentations in college, and spend middle school in computer labs playing *Oregon Trail*. They organized for the Jena Six on Facebook when you still needed a school email address for access.[13] They created online social networks about Black hair in the Black blogosphere. They grew up with digital culture the way that hip-hop feminists grew up with hip-hop. Not all Black women born in the hip-hop era are hip-hop feminists, just as not all Black women coming of age with digital technology are digital Black feminists. But falling in love with digital technology, just like falling in love with hip-hop, afforded new possibilities and set up new barriers for crafting Black feminist principles and praxes. Both hip-hop feminists and digital Black feminists have watched the relationship they formed with their crib mate shift based on an injection of money. When digital Black feminists fell in love with digital culture, the consumption of Black feminism online transformed self-care, intersectionality, accountability, and the traditions of Black oral culture into products. While we laud the work of digital Black feminists in creating new possibilities using their technological skills, we must also consider the potential long-term implications of this relationship.

# Conclusion

*A Digital Black Feminist Future*

In June and July of 2020, the country was in the midst of a pandemic. The novel coronavirus (COVID-19) had killed more than 140,000 Americans, and millions were left unemployed as municipalities shuttered restaurants and stores trying to curb the spread of the virus. Black and Latino/a Americans were twice as likely to die from the virus and were infected at three times the rate of white Americans (Oppel et al., 2020). The unemployment rate remained 5 percent higher for Black workers than the overall unemployment rate in June of 2020 (Ziv, 2020). Under the forty-fifth president's leadership, the federal government lied about the rise in cases and deprived state governments of the resources needed to combat the outbreak. At the same time, people took to the streets for weeks in support of Black lives. In June, a Minneapolis high school senior recorded the murder of George Floyd by Minneapolis police officers on video for the world to see. The nine-minute video showed officer Derek Chauvin and three other officers deprive Floyd of air, holding him to the ground as the public watched without recourse. In the same period, Ahmaud Arbery, a twenty-five-year-old Black man in Georgia, was chased and killed by a group of white men. His murder was also captured on video. Breonna Taylor was shot to death by police in March of 2020 as she slept in her home. The district attorney and law enforcement's refusal to hold officers accountable revived the circumstances of her murder during the uprisings in June and July. After weeks of protests across the country, officers were charged in the death of Floyd, and Arbery's killers were arrested. In Kentucky, policy makers passed legislation bearing Taylor's name, even as her killers remained on the police force facing no consequences. In the same weeks, corporations began removing racist imagery like from their pancake boxes and professional football teams. Mayors in DC, New York, and Oakland painted "Black Lives Matter" on their streets. The country promised, again, to engage in serious discussions about police brutality and systemic racism.

While protests grew throughout the country, Donald Trump ordered tear gas to be shot at peaceful protesters to clear his path for a photo op outside a church. While people across the globe marched for Black lives, a young activist named Oluwatoyin Salau was sexually assaulted and killed by a Black man in Tallahassee who promised her shelter and protection. Days after authorities found her body, rapper J. Cole released a song suggesting Black women change their tone if they want Black men to be better allies and become more informed about Black liberation.[1] When taken as a whole, these weeks' events felt unreal, unprecedented, and terrifying while simultaneously too familiar. In these weeks, like every other week in America, Black women fought anti-Black racism from the state while demanding that assault and violence perpetrated by Black men be taken seriously. Online, many digital Black feminists used their platforms to advocate for themselves and demand their Freedom as a necessary step in the path to liberation for all.

Interviewed in the weeks that followed the deaths of Taylor and Floyd, Brittney Cooper explained,

> You know, we have this thing in feminist theory where we say, The public sphere is traditionally the sphere of men and the private sphere is traditionally the sphere of women and, of course, we mean white men and white women. So what Black folks are outraged about is that the public sphere is not a sphere that is particularly hospitable to Black men. But we do not react as vehemently when we learn that the private sphere is not a sphere that's hospitable to Black women (Burnley, 2020).

Cooper is pointing out the palatable outrage rightly expressed when police officers murder Black men in the streets. She reminds us, though, that Black women are often killed in homes where they sleep—by officers or intimate partners. Black women organized on and offline to demand justice and accountability in the prominent cases of police brutality in the news. But Breonna Taylor's, Oluwatoyin Salau's, and Priscilla Slater's names did not draw the same attention as the Black men killed on video.[2] These women were killed in either a home or an incident of domestic violence—in what we would consider a private sphere. The deaths of these Black women do not evoke the same reaction as their Black male counterparts. Just as the cult of true womanhood established a century earlier, Black women do not have a right to the private world of the home or the public world of white men. We do not have a framework to understand Black women's pain and death or to see them as rightfully occupying space in our society.

Digital Black feminists, through their principles, through their praxes, and ultimately in their products, demand such a space for Black women, not just in death—but to celebrate and experience the fullness of life. One of the significant lessons in how digital Black feminists approach their work is that they occupy spaces not reserved for or considered appropriate for them. Ultimately, digital Black feminism centers Black women, not just in online spaces, but in our discussion about freedom, technology, justice, and American society. Instead of navigating a world where they must justify their existence, thoughts, and experiences, the virtual beauty shop at once grants independence and a historical commitment to writing, blogging, and creating for themselves. They create a space that is not concerned with the gaze or affirmation of others. Ironically, this is the reason the public must pay attention. Black folks' redeployment, reconception, and recreation of technology is not an effort to teach white America what to do with digital tools.[3] As writer Damon Young explained to CNN, "I don't write with the intent of explaining race and racism to White people. I write to articulate and better understand the circus in and outside of my head. I write for catharsis. I write to challenge myself. I write to entertain myself. . . . But their education is incidental—the rub, not the steak. And perhaps that's the lesson. That my world revolves around me, not them" (Blake, 2020). Outside of the dominant group's gaze, Black writers are at the center of their own world, and within this space, their creativity is not limited by the white imagination.

In the introduction, I asked if Black women were magic and mused about the refrain that Black women should save us all. If not evident through the words of the digital Black feminists I cite in this text, the answer is no. Feminista Jones describes the move to valorize Black women online after the 2016 election this way: "Rather than be honorably heralded for our brilliance, fortitude, and moxie, we became a frontline barrier to protect and guide those who were suddenly beginning to get an inkling sense of what it might be like to be subjected to perpetual oppression, or at least limitations on and boundaries around one's freedom" (Jones, 2019a, p. 149). Perhaps the Trump presidency's only valuable feature is how apparent the blatant disregard for American citizens is by this administration and those who support it. Trump undermines democratic principles daily, and his explicit narcissistic calculations make the faults in the American system of democracy more apparent to those most invested in it. Trump's presidency has forced many white Americans to confront how systems erected with them in mind will actively destroy them if they do not fall in line. Black folks have never had the luxury to imagine the U.S. as a bastion of freedom. As Nikole Hannah-Jones (2019), founder of the 1619 Project, writes, "Black people have been the perfecters of this democracy." This does not mean Black folks are required to take on this burden on behalf of the entire nation. While holding the U.S. accountable for its broken systems and promises, Black women are about the business of saving themselves. The work of digital Black feminism is to center Black women and nonbinary folks. In doing this, they remind all those who bear witness that a nation that would marginalize them is an incomplete construction of our possibilities as a country. Digital Black feminists demand a space that revolves around Black women. Black feminism does not exist to correct white feminism, the beauty shop is not a derivative of the barbershop, and Black feminist technoculture is not defined through its resistance to white technoculture. The critical lesson of Black feminist technoculture is that we stop using whiteness as the lens through which we examine technology and maleness as the lens through which we examine Blackness. When we lift those limitations, Black feminist technoculture provides an essential tool for understanding digital technology and society.

Digital Black feminism places Black feminist thought in conversation with digital studies. A new generation of Black feminists has reconceived Black feminism by redefining our relationship to technology. In chapter 1, I traced Black American women's long relationship with technology, beginning in the antebellum South. While some have described technology as a product of white Western culture, by unsettling the term's origins in common vernacular, we see that Black women were never divorced from technology. Instead, we were intentionally written out of history. The work of this text places Black women back at the center of our discourse about technology and uses that starting place to examine the trajectory of Black feminist thought. From there, we see digital Black feminism within a tradition of Black women's mastery of technical skills.

As Maria del Guadalupe Davidson explains, "If Black feminism is going to live up to its emancipatory potential, it must let go of its scripted, safe, and bounded actuality. . . . It is by restoring the multiplicity, plasticity, and dynamism of Black feminist theory that it can reclaim its status as an emancipatory praxis" (Davidson, 2019, p. 111). Digital Black feminists contribute a new emphasis on principles like agency and the right to self-identify and question and trouble any iteration of feminist thought that is not freeing for all Black women. Just as digital culture troubles binaries like work and play, private and public, digital Black feminists trouble gender and sexual binaries. Because of online publishing demands, they are forced into and embrace complicated allegiances with allies and tech companies. Their relationship with digital production allows digital Black feminists to sit comfortably within a dialectic of self and community interests. Doing digital Black feminism draws on centuries-long relationships Black women writers have with notions of capture and the power of who tells Black women's stories. They chart new avenues for publishing but meet many of the same roadblocks of Black feminists of the nineteenth and twentieth centuries. They stitch and thread together theory with praxis extend to the emancipatory work of their feminist foremothers.

Digital Black feminists are also constricted in serious ways by technology through ownership, bias, and platform design. Black folks, like everyone else, must contend with destructive relationships with capitalism and technology. As digital Black feminism becomes a commodity, its revolutionary potential is tested. The marriage of capitalism and technology in digital environments creates circumstances where digital Black feminists may have ideals and practices in conflict, just like anyone else. On July 7, 2020, organizers released an event flyer on Twitter featuring artists, journalists, academics, politicians, and activists for a live broadcast called "#SayHerName: Justice for Breonna Taylor" set to air on Players TV and stream live online the following day.

Some users immediately critiqued those involved as using Taylor's death to promote themselves. Others pointed out that no Louisville

Figure C.1. Justice for Breonna Taylor flyer distributed on Twitter, July 7, 2020.
Screenshot by author.

organizers were present on the flyer. The design decentered Taylor and
instead prominently featured the images of participants in the dialogue. As one anonymous user tweeted, "This picture really bothers
me. Someone should have said center Breonna Taylor. She seems like
an afterthought. Design really matters in stuff like this" (This picture
really bothers me, 2020). The public is becoming more aware of how
digital technology is deeply connected to capitalism and is holding Black
organizers accountable for any perception of "grifting." Many of those
involved in this event, like scholar Brittney Cooper and activists Alicia
Garza and Brittany Packnett Cunningham, have long resumes of work

on behalf of Black women. It would be difficult to contextualize this event as a "grift." But no matter the organizers' intent, users responded to the possibility that someone was using a Black woman's death for financial or personal gain.

As digital Black feminists navigate social media for its liberatory potential, they are not immune from influencer and celebrity culture or the demands of digital technology. Within a digital ecosystem, followers, engagement, and self-promotion are paramount. As the chapters in this book outline, at each stage of their relationship with technology, Black women and Black feminists have had to navigate tools used for control and violence. At every stage, they have manipulated those tools to their benefit. Nevertheless, they have also adopted practices that could, when left unchecked, restrict their liberatory potential. Uncritical praise of digital Black feminism is not a useful enterprise. Instead, researchers and activists must be deeply critical of how new instantiations of Black feminist theory and praxis are connected to the digital culture in which they are conceived and its impact on their efficacy. In this text, I sought to temper effusive praise of Black women with the reality that Black women, like everyone else, are met with systems constructed to diminish our capacity to do revolutionary work.

While I am committed to doing critical work that unpacks these nuances, one contribution I hope this text makes to future researchers is a commitment to the people at the center of the work. Black feminism online is both personal and public and, as such, requires intention and care around method and ethics. As Sarah Florini reminds us, the study of marginalized groups requires "humility and a deep commitment to ethics" (Florini, 2019, p. 186). Thanks to archivists' labor, the work of Black feminist thinkers like Zora Neale Hurston or Anna Julia Cooper is not only available but curated to organize the different corners of their lives. Their personal papers like diaries and letters are separated from public speeches and essays. Working in a digital era, researchers must wade through the tweets, blog posts, and videos of public scholars and writers and determine what constitutes their public work versus personal and private dialogue in a public venue. It is not sufficient, from my perspective, to consider all work available to the public as public work. Sorting the different expectations of consumption of publicly available materials for individuals and groups is beyond the requirements of institutional review boards. I argue, though, that this is a necessity of ethical research. I am not confident I have always gotten this right. However, like the work of the digital Black feminists I write about, I seek Black women's liberation, and I intend that nothing I write advances my career while causing harm to other Black women. I take caution in whom I cite, which tweets or stories I share, and how much personal information shared in other digital forums I repeat in this text. Countless people participated in the dialogue in the blogosphere and on social media that shaped digital Black feminism. In this text, I choose to cite and publicize the work of those who through their public writing, signal a willingness to enter the public discourse on issues of race and gender. I treat these public intellectuals, writers, and users of digital technology as experts in their field. Digital Black feminists, who choose to make their work product accessible, should be appropriately cited and credited for their work. Their public work should not bring gain to researchers who are unwilling to see them as partners in their research enterprise.

In writing this book, I intend to send up a flare to those who study and report on digital culture about the glaring absence of Black women in their work. For those studying online harassment and trolling, algorithmic bias, and digital activism, Black women must be included in your work. As Sarah Florini concludes in her book *Beyond Hashtags*, "There is a direct link from trolls harassing Black feminists on Twitter in 2012 to the emergence of the 'Alt-Right'" (Florini, 2019, p. 186). The 2016 election outcome might have been different if politicians and the public took Black women's treatment online and their strategies for digital survival seriously. Excluding Black women or treating Black people as a monolith makes research on digital culture incomplete. It does not provide us a way to understand the reaches and limitations of our digital tools. It misses the rhetorical craft of those who must navigate being both the "mules"[4] and the ignored technophiles of society. Beyond incorporating more Black women as research subjects, Black feminism provides a new lens to understand the digital culture. Digital Black feminist thought challenges notions of agency, privacy, community, and digital praxis with implications reaching to academic research, politics, journalism, and beyond.

While working on this book, my seven-year-old son asked what it was about. After patiently listening to explanations each day and asking many insightful questions, he summarized his understanding with a simple assessment: "So it's complicated." He was right. Studying digital culture ethically and documenting Black feminist thought's transformation produce complications, many of which I could not take up in this text. The intersection between patriarchy and white supremacy is complicated, as are the principles and praxes digital Black feminists have established to deal with these oppressive forces. Understanding the joys and labors of Black women, their fight for liberation, and their complicity in systems of capitalism is very complicated. Digital Black feminism is complicated, but perhaps this sheds light on why this inquiry is necessary. Like Joan Morgan, I think there is merit to "fuck[ing] with the grays."

This book gave me the space to deal with a subject matter very personal to me. My Black feminism was born of reading Joan Morgan and Patricia Hill Collins in undergrad and cultivated online in the Black blogosphere of the early 2000s. So in addition to academic inquiry, I am also attempting to reconcile my mixed feelings about watching digital Black feminism grow up. This text documents the move from digital Black feminist enclaved communities of the blogosphere to having our ideas taken up in a digital marketplace. Black feminist technoculture is now on display for the whole world to see. It is immensely gratifying to see Black feminist writers treated with the professionalism they deserve. Writers who had small blogs in the early 2000s now have book deals, are being interviewed by major news channels and publications, and are starting new podcasts and media companies. But publicity for digital Black feminism means we must navigate this new world where our voices and thoughts are visible beyond the enclaves of blogs and the Twitterverse. And really, it is complicated.

# ACKNOWLEDGMENTS

I want to thank my family, who extended me so much grace as I worked on his book. To my partner in this life, whose support is beyond measure, thanks for the big stuff and the small, for believing my work is valuable and doing whatever necessary to give me the space to do it. And in doing this, John, thank you for teaching our kids how to stand next to someone, how to walk alongside them, how to make decisions together, and how to provide your partner the love and freedom to grow into exactly who they must be.

Thank you to my children, Jalen and Micah, for your patience with Mommy. I love being your mom, and being your mom makes me a better scholar, teacher, and writer. I'm so proud of who you are already and cannot wait to see who you grow to be.

Thank you to my Knight and Steele families for your support and love. A special thank you to my mother, Bethany, and mother-in-love, Debbie, who have cooked for me, watched kiddos, and poured their love into me throughout this writing process. Mom, you have provided me with what you didn't have. You made sure I always knew who I was. I am forever grateful to be your daughter. Thank you to my dad, who is not here to see this book completed but whose spirit I carry with me each day.

To Kristi and Tiffany—my chosen family—who saw the lowest and most challenging days of this process and held my hand throughout. I love you.

I want to thank all the women of BBRDC, who inspire me, hold me up, and cheer me on every day. I consider myself fortunate to be surrounded by their brilliance, their wit, and their beauty.

I am grateful for Dr. Debra Davis, whose patience, expertise, and compassion have helped me push forward, strengthen my resolve, grant myself grace, and provide myself care.

Thank you to my colleagues, friends, and writing crew André Brock, Sarah Florini, Kishonna Gray, Jessica Lu, Miriam Sweeney, and Kevin

Winstead for providing advice, encouragement, and the kind of back channel everyone needs in their life—especially to Dre and Sarah, whose work makes my own writing possible. Thank you for laying the foundation for the kind of Black digital scholarship I hope to achieve.

Thank you to my friend and mentor Safiya Noble for your guidance through this process. I promise to always pay it forward.

I am grateful for the support of my department and colleagues at the University of Maryland and to the many interlocutors of AADHum—the students, faculty, librarians, archivists, and community groups whose work inspired me for three years. Thank you for teaching me the importance of the archive and slow work and holding me to my principles and values. My work with these amazing scholars changed the trajectory of this book.

I am thankful for the entire editorial team at NYU Press for your labor and support throughout this process, including the series editors for Critical Cultural Communication. A special note of gratitude to Aswin Punathambekar, who first read and supported my proposal; to Eric Zinner for his thoughtful stewardship; and to Furqan Sayeed for his diligence. Thank you to Scribe Inc. and Ideas of Fire as well for their editing and indexing work. The gorgeous cover for this book features the work of Lavett Ballard. Thank you for allowing *The Caretakers* to help tell the story of Digital Black Feminism.

The work of Black feminist writers is my lifeblood. There are far too many to acknowledge here, but I am so grateful that Black women have always found a way to leave a record for ourselves. I am grateful for those whose voices were silenced in our histories, yet their love, labor, and abundant joy runs through their descendants.

I am forever grateful for Patricia Hill Collins, Joan Morgan, and Anna Everett, whose theoretical work is the basis for this book.

Finally, I thank the Black women writers, bloggers, tweeters, and digital public scholars whose work I am fortunate to chart in this book. I found the blogosphere when I was not yet sure what I would be doing with my life. I found a community of Black folks and Black women online during a period when I did not have one offline. Your words, humor, care, and digital Black feminism changed my life. Thank you for letting me write about it.

# NOTES

## INTRODUCTION

1 *African American* refers to a group of Americans who trace their ancestry through chattel slavery and whose cultural legacy intermingles traditions from the continent of Africa with those of the United States. *Black* refers to members of the African diaspora categorized as Black by laws and social norms within a binary system of racial stratification in the U.S. African Americans are therefore considered Black by the author of this study. However, *Black* may encompass members of the African diaspora who live in the U.S. but are from other parts of the world and do not trace their lineage through chattel slavery in the Americas. Because the terms are related and often used interchangeably, I will use the writer's or speaker's preference when available. In all other cases, I will use *Black* to refer to (1) a system of categorization based on phenotype and (2) a chosen identity and shared historical and cultural experience based on that categorization but also formed with Black people's agency.

2 *Misogynoir* is a term coined by Moya Bailey. Bailey describes misogynoir as "the anti-Black racist misogyny that Black women experience, particularly in US visual and digital culture. . . . Misogynoir describes the uniquely co-constitutive racialized and sexist violence that befalls Black women as a result of their simultaneously and interlocking oppression at the intersection of racial and gender marginalization" (Bailey, 2021, p. 1).

3 Donald Trump was elected as the forty-fifth president of the U.S. by the Electoral College in 2016 despite losing the popular vote to Hillary Rodham Clinton by more than three million votes.

4 *Insecure* is a television show that is produced by Issa Rae and airs on HBO. Two of the primary characters on the show, Lawrence and Issa, have been involved in the multiple-season arc in which their romantic future is unknown. Fans of the show have created live-watching sessions online using hashtags like #Insecure, #TeamLawrence, #TeamIssa, and #SoInsecurr to discuss the relationships on the show in connection to broader themes of Black love.

5 Chapter 2 provides an extended explanation of the origins of hip-hop feminism and how digital Black feminism springs from this iteration of Black feminist praxis.

6 Brock's critical technocultural discourse analysis (CTDA) provides the basis of this methodological approach to the study of Black discourse online. CTDA as

conceptualized by Brock is an approach to critical study of discourse and technology. As Brock explains, CTDA is "an intervention into normative and analytic technology analyses, as CTDA formulates technology as cultural representations and social structures in order to simultaneously interrogate culture and technology as intertwined concepts" (Brock, 2018, p. 1012).

7 Following third-wave feminism, which was more attentive to issues of race, ethnicity, and socioeconomic status, some scholars argue fourth-wave feminism builds upon this trajectory while doing so online. Online blogs and news magazines have begun differentiating this fourth wave as sex positive, transinclusive, and happening in an era of #MeToo (Cochrane, 2013; Grady, 2018; Sollee, 2015). Writing for the Political Studies Association, Ealasaid Munro considers the possibility that the internet is itself responsible for cultural shifts leading to a new wave of feminism (Munro, 2013). Accepting that feminism falls within "waves" requires certain assumptions about continuity and congruence between different people engaged in gender activism. Even if unintentionally, the pursuit of a new "wave" of feminism also places mainstream white feminism as normative by tracing a lineage of feminist thought through white women's work.

## CHAPTER 1. A HISTORY OF BLACK WOMEN AND TECHNOLOGY, OR BADGES OF OPPRESSION AND POSITIONS OF STRENGTH

1 Kathleen Brown explains, "Compared to the stirring narratives of emancipation that defined the histories of women's rights, abolition, and the civil rights movement, or even of the Revolution itself, early America could boast relatively little collective political activity arising from historical subjects' consciousness of their identities as Anglo-American women or as African-American men and women" (K. M. Brown, 1998, p. 99).

2 In this text, when referencing Africans held in slavery in the U.S., I refrain from the terms *slave* and *slave owner*. While no terminology undoes the violence done in validating the fiction that one person can rightfully own another, I attempt to honor the humanity of our ancestors by writing about them as men, women, and people who are enslaved rather than as slaves. Likewise, I replace the terms *slave owner* and *master* with *enslaver*. Changing this terminology is a conscious effort to disrupt our passive acceptance of these terrorist activities.

3 Sarah Boone improved upon the design of the ironing board. Though she was once enslaved, she went on to hold the patent on her invention in 1892. Ellen Elgin invented the clothes wringer in 1888 but never received profits for her invention. Miriam E. Benjamin invented the gong and signal chair in 1888, a precursor to a call button on an airplane. In the same year, Sarah Goode was granted a patent for the cabinet bed (a bed that folded out into a writing desk). Only four Black women were granted patents between the end of the Civil War and 1900 (McNeill, 2017). We will never know how many more had their inventions stolen.

4  Originally transcribed by Marius Robinson in 1851, the speech by Truth does not contain the line "Ain't I a woman," the southern dialect, the mention of thirteen children, or the lashes written in the 1863 version by woman's suffragist Frances Dana Barker Gage (Brezina, 2005; Mabee & Newhouse, 1995). Gage's version, published a full twelve years after the speech was originally given, inserts new elements meant to activate common tropes about slavery and likely exaggerates the audience's response as negative (Mabee & Newhouse, 1995). The original account provided by Robinson of Truth's speech still makes the case that Black women, because of their unique position, were too often disregarded in the struggle for both abolition and women's suffrage.

5  The misattribution of the word *ain't* to Truth demonstrates how the very words of Black women advocating for their own freedom are not thought sufficient by some allies. In recasting Truth's words in stereotypical southern slave vernacular, the white suffragist writer and abolitionist Frances Dana Barker Gage creates a caricature in place of the fully capable and complex Truth.

6  Defined by Lisa A. Keister and Darby E. Southgate, the cult of domesticity was a "value system in white upper- and middleclass homes in the United States during the nineteenth century that emphasized women's embodiment of virtue" (Keister & Southgate, 2012, p. 228).

7  Joan Morgan (2000) deconstructs the myth of the Strong Black Woman in the book *When Chickenheads Come Home to Roost*. She argues this mythology around Black women as unemotional pillars of strength allows for their feelings, pain, and harms to be discarded not only by individuals but also by laws and policies making it easier to violate Black women's bodies.

8  African American culture has been maintained in the preservation of oral culture. Primary oral cultures are those untouched by literacy and writing. Orality has implications for knowledge and recall and possesses several salient features. In a primary oral culture, a person can know only as much as she can recall, making mnemonics important cognitive and social tools and proverbs emerge as means to evaluate decisions. Oral cultures tend to be additive in discourse rather than subordinative. Aggregate expressions are taken in total (sturdy oak, glorious revolution). Literacy separates into nouns and adjectives what oral cultures understand as whole ideas. Oral cultures also rely on tradition more heavily to preserve knowledge over time. This leads to respect and near worship of those "wise experts" who serve as guardians of the culture's truth. Oral cultures are not objective but empathic in their speech. Since there is no written record, they can disregard those things that cause conflict or discrepancy. The interiority of sound places man at the center of his universe within a society of primary orality. These features separate oral cultures from print-based cultures (Ong, 1982).

9  Refused the right to read by law, enslaved Africans living in the U.S. developed pidgin languages for survival that eventually became creoles. These languages that combined West African words and grammatical structure with Victorian English

and French are indicative of not only survival but the ability to create and generate new knowledge when presented with obstacles.

10 In popular English vernacular, the term *signifying* refers to denotation of meaning through the use of a sign or word. Within the African American community, the term generally refers to a verbal contest where the most imaginative user of indirection, irony, and insult wins (Lee, 1993). See chapter 5 for more on signifyin'.

11 Tweet citations without URLs come from accounts that have since gone private (but were public at the time) or where the tweet is otherwise no longer accessible.

12 As Jessica Lu details, the Freedmen's Bureau was charged with "facilitate[ing] the transition of emancipated slaves from bondage to freedom" and was "empowered to control" Black free person's behaviors post–Civil War. The bureau dictated that immorality in the form of living together without legal marriage was not appropriate behavior for those seeking to hold on to the "freedom which [had] been purchased for [emancipated slaves] in blood and treasure" (J. H. Lu, 2017, pp. 1–2, 131).

13 Black women online use rhetorical arguments about financial agency in similar ways that draw similar critiques. See chapter 3 on the principle of agency for digital Black feminists.

## CHAPTER 2. BLACK FEMINIST TECHNOCULTURE, OR *THE VIRTUAL BEAUTY SHOP*

1 The *big chop* is a term in Black hair communities that signifies cutting off chemically processed or damaged hair, leaving behind natural hair (N. Walton & Carter, 2013).

2 Extending the work of Nancy Fraser (1990) on subaltern counterpublics, Catherine Squires (2002) contends that Black alternate publics should be classified as counterpublics, enclaves, and satellites. Counterpublics seek engagement with the dominant group. According to Squires, this does not sufficiently address how and why some groups form and their practices for engagement.

3 Tignon is a type of cloth covering worn over the head. Tignon laws, enacted in Louisiana during the Spanish colonial period, required women of African descent to cover their heads.

4 According to Crystal Abidin, influencers are "everyday ordinary Internet users who accumulate a relatively large following on blogs and social media through the textual and visual narration of their personal lives and lifestyles, engage with their following in 'digital' and 'physical' spaces, and monetize their following by integrating 'advertorials' into their blogs or social media posts, and making physical paid-guest appearances at events" (Abidin, 2016, p. 3).

5 Patterns of interaction across online platforms signal a shift back to orality (December, 1993; Fowler, 1994; Rheingold, 2000).

6 Scholars like Lisa Nakamura, Anna Everett, Adam Banks, and André Brock writing about race and Blackness online contradicted the digital divide as the only mechanism by which to consider marginalized communities and the internet.

They did this work with a deep and abiding commitment to Black lives. Recently, however, with the popularity of Black Twitter and the use of Black social networking sites as mechanisms to coordinate around social movements, Black internet studies has exploded.

7 See Bellinger, 2007; Byrd & Tharps, 2014; Patton, 2006; Robinson, 2011; S. Tate, 2007; and Thompson, 2009.

8 As Nina Banks writes for the Economic Policy Institute, "Compared with other women in the United States, Black women have always had the highest levels of labor market participation regardless of age, marital status, or presence of children at home. In 1880, 35.4 percent of married black women and 73.3 percent of single black women were in the labor force compared with only 7.3 percent of married white women and 23.8 percent of single white women. Black women's higher participation rates extended over their lifetimes, even after marriage, while white women typically left the labor force after marriage" (N. Banks, 2019, para. 3).

9 In a 2014 discussion at the New School in New York City, cultural critic and Black feminist writer bell hooks said, "I see a part of Beyoncé that is, in fact, anti-feminist—that is, a terrorist—especially in terms of the impact on young girls" (King, 2014, para. 1).

10 *Lemonade* was a visual album released by singer and songwriter Beyoncé Knowles-Carter in 2016. The album received widespread praise for the deeply personal music with references to Knowles-Carter's marriage and relationship with her father and husband. Additionally, the album garnered attention for the visual references to African and Africanist imagery. The album also reignited the controversy around Knowles-Carter's use of the term *feminist* to describe herself.

11 *Hotep* can be described as faux pan-Africanism laden with misogyny and homophobia. André Brock describes *hotep* as "fundamentalist misogynist respectability" (Brock, 2020, p. 173), while Damon Young (2016) explains that while the term should seemingly have a positive connotation, it has come to be an "all-encompassing term describing a person who's either a clueless parody of Afrocentricity . . . or someone who's loudly, conspicuously and obnoxiously pro-Black but anti-progress."

## CHAPTER 3. PRINCIPLES FOR A DIGITAL BLACK FEMINISM, OR BLOGGING WHILE BLACK

1 A derivative of blogs (text-based web logs), vlogs are video blogs, which combine video content with image and supporting texts.

2 In 2004, Google purchased Blogger, making it more well known and accessible to the public. Blogger blogs, now hosted by Google, are accessed from a subdomain of blogspot.com.

3 *Black Twitter* is a term used to refer to the overrepresentation of African Americans on the social media platform and the tendency to use hashtags and elicit trending topics that are directly connected to the Black community (Sharma,

2013). Research suggests that "Black Twitter" is a phenomenon cultivated by a group of Twitter users who use the platform differently than many others. Based on the history of African American's connection to oral communication and performative wordplay, "Twitter's architecture creates participant structures that accommodate the crucial function of the audience during signifyin'" (Florini, 2013, p. 10).

4  Twitter's application programming interface (API) allows you to gain access to a high volume of tweets on specific subjects.

5  The *Root* launched in 2008 and is an African American digital magazine.

6  In the film *What's Love Got to Do with It*, an abusive Ike Turner demonstrates his dominance over his wife, forcefully making her eat cake in a restaurant. The pivotal scene shows the audience but one example of his physical abuse of his wife, Tina Turner, whose given name was Anna Mae Bullock. In Beyoncé's song "Drunk in Love," Jay-Z uses the line "Eat the cake, Anna Mae," taken from the film, to refer to a consensual sex act.

7  BlackPlanet is one of the longest running Black social networking sites. Founded in 1999, the site had more than fifteen million users registered by 2007 (Byrne, 2007).

8  Postraciality, as exemplified in the lead-up to the Obama presidency, suggests that because of the economic progress or individual political success of some African Americans, race is no longer a factor determining the life success of groups. Postraciality as an ideological racial project (see Omi & Winant, 1998) seeks to undermine policies like affirmative action, insisting that government and institutions are not responsible to undue generations of discrimination and oppression.

9  Eduardo Bonilla-Silva (2006) describes *reverse racism* as a term within a color-blind framework that seeks to minimize and deflect from a discussion of institutional and systemic racism, which possesses material consequences on Black and brown people in America.

10  Hate violence crimes are those motivated by bias or based on the victim's perceived membership in a specific group, such as race, national origin, sexual orientation, gender, or religious belief.

11  Monica Roberts passed away before the publication of this book. I am grateful for the words and legacy she left behind.

12  Janet Mock is a writer, director, and activist who has used her platform to advocate for trans rights. Mock wrote the best-selling memoir *Redefining Realness*, which was a *New York Times* best seller. She now serves as a producer and director on the hit show *Pose*, which focuses on trans and queer ball culture in the 1980s and 1990s.

13  Laverne Cox is an actress and advocate. She was the first openly trans actress to be nominated for an Emmy Award.

14  Jezebel's target audience is women. Launched in 2007, the website's tagline is "Celebrity, Sex, Fashion for Women. Without Airbrushing."

15  The *Root* launched in 2008 as an online magazine for African Americans.

16  The *Onion* is a satirical newspaper that exists both online and in print.

17 Kinja is free online news aggregator, launched in April 2004. It is operated by Gizmodo Media Group.

18 In August of 2017, Jackson wrote a deeply personal essay about the impact of the Trump presidency in bringing deeply rooted issues of race to the surface in his relationship with his white mother. The essay was republished in other online magazines, and Jackson went on to give interviews about the topic of his upbringing as a Black person with a white mother. While Jackson had written about his mother in the past, this essay published across multiple platforms appeared to gain more traction than those that came before.

19 According to their website, "#BlackLivesMatter was founded in 2013 in response to the acquittal of Trayvon Martin's murderer. Black Lives Matter Foundation, Inc is a global organization in the US, UK, and Canada, whose mission is to eradicate white supremacy and build local power to intervene in violence inflicted on Black communities by the state and vigilantes. By combating and countering acts of violence, creating space for Black imagination and innovation, and centering Black joy, we are winning immediate improvements in our lives" (https://blacklivesmatter.com).

20 According to their website, the Movement for Black Lives formed in 2014 to "as a space for Black organizations across the country to debate and discuss the current political conditions, develop shared assessments of what political interventions were necessary in order to achieve key policy, cultural and political wins, convene organizational leadership in order to debate and co-create a shared movement wide strategy" (https://m4bl.org).

21 Former social worker, activist, and writer Feminista Jones created the hashtag #YouOKSis to call attention to specific street harassment of Black women and the mechanisms other women use to act in solidarity and intervene (when possible).

## CHAPTER 4. DIGITAL BLACK FEMINIST PRAXIS, OR MAVIS BEACON TEACHES TYPING

1 The *Seattle Times* reported that her name was taken from Mavis Staples, a favorite singer of the creator, and *beacon*, a word that means "to light the way" (Macklin, 1995).

2 Harold Innis explains that unlike time-based media (like the voice) space-based media, like the printed word, extend influence and therefore facilitate rapid change, development, and "progress." In the U.S., the dominant group's emphasis on space-based media links our mode of communication to our quest for dominance, order, and power. The U.S. was built and expanded with an emphasis on paper and literacy. The embrace of space-based media heavily influences the structure of the government, our relationship to religion, and our creation of hierarchical systems of power distribution and social organization.

3 By 1822, Thomas Pinckney, a Revolutionary War hero charged with identifying how Denmark Vesey was able to plot an insurrection, explained that literacy and the growing ability of those enslaved persons to communicate among each other

were threats that likely could no longer be stopped, for literacy had indeed spread too far (Ford, 2009).

4 Out of print for more than thirty years, *Their Eyes Were Watching God* is a novel that traces the life of the main character, Janie Crawford, a southern Black woman in the 1930s.

5 Luvvie Ajayi is a writer who began her career in the blogosphere. Her writing has since catapulted her to a public stage. Ajayi gained national attention for her recaps of the popular television series *Scandal* when show creator Shonda Rhimes became a fan. Ajayi parlayed this media attention into two podcasts, one that she records with television star and friend Yvonne Orji and another, *Rants and Randomness*, that focuses on pop culture. Ajayi is a *New York Times* best-selling author, with her book *I'm Judging You* the winner of multiple awards. Ajayi grew up in Chicago and was born in Nigeria. In addition to her public writing and speaking, the author and Ted Talks speaker offers classes on marketing and branding.

6 Facebook is the parent company of Instagram.

7 As André Brock explains, "For Black culture, the invocation of ratchet conjures up someone who has no filter or propriety; a condition that across American race relations has often been akin to a death sentence. Ratchet shares connotative space with ghetto but differs from ghetto's aesthetics thanks to its enactment and performance of militant insouciance" (Brock, 2020, p. 128).

Brock defines *ratchetry* in the following way:

> I appropriated the term ratchet to ground this frame in the banal, sensual, and outspoken aspects of Black expressive culture. A second and third reason for using the term lies within the technical and technocultural denotations of ratchet. Technically, a ratchet is a device that, once engaged, can only rotate in one direction, while technoculturally, ratchet describes a process that is changing irreversibly or deteriorating. The multiple dimensions of ratchet offer a directional, agentive, and technical identity that works well for this frame. Finally, it is my firm belief that before commodification and before resistance, Black folk enact their cultural identity online because they enjoy being Black; my definition of ratchetry thus includes a libidinal component of pleasure. In all cases, ratchet indicates a change agent—one that seems inexorable and unamenable once involved. (Brock, 2020, p. 126)

8 As Mary Helen Washington explains, Cooper "is never able to discard the ethics of true womanhood, and except for one passage about Black laundry women, she does not imagine ordinary Black working women as the basis of her feminist praxis" (Washington, 1987, p. xlvi).

9 See Alexander-Floyd, 2012; Guy-Sheftall, 2009; May, 2008, 2009; and Moody-Turner, 2019.

10 In addition to enclave and counterpublics, Squires offers that the Black community also forms satellite publics. Satellites seek spaces separate from the dominant group but engage with other publics when necessary. They do so not for purposes

of physical protection like enclaves but in order to keep their cultural identities intact (Squires, 2002).

11 *Gradient Lair* is a self-described womanist blog discussing art, media, social media, sociopolitics, and culture (www.gradientlair.com).

12 Notably, Jim DeRogatis of the *Chicago Sun-Times* has written about Kelly's abuse of Black women and girls for over twenty years. Multiple survivors also came forward over the years to tell their stories.

13 *Surviving R. Kelly* was a multipart docuseries aired on Lifetime. The program, which aired in 2019, documented the decades of sexual abuse perpetrated on Black women and girls by celebrated R&B singer and songwriter R. Kelly. *Surviving R. Kelly* featured survivors recounting their experiences in their own words in addition to celebrities and activists.

14 Virtual agents are computer programs and interfaces that are designed to have human features, characteristics, and personality traits.

## CHAPTER 5. DIGITAL BLACK FEMINISM AS A PRODUCT, OR "IT'S FUNNY HOW MONEY CHANGE A SITUATION"

1 A GIF (graphics interchange format) is a series of images or soundless videos played in a loop continuously. Social media users popularized GIFs, which are two to five seconds in length, to add context, emotion, and reaction to their messages.

2 See Brock (2020) for more on Black discursive play and libidinal economy.

3 Mighty Networks is a website / app development software that allows content creators to create paid or unpaid apps/sites. They describe their software as key for brand development and community creation for "deep interests."

4 Here I use the term *engagement* not as a measure of the level of interest or commitment from an audience but as a tool advertisers use to measure how often something is seen, shared, commented on, or liked.

5 In the years 2016–19, BuzzFeed—an American internet media, news, and entertainment company with a focus on digital media—published multiple checklists to test one's level of "wokeness" while commodifying ideas from Black feminist thought, including the following: "How Woke Are You?," "How Much of a Feminist Are You?," and "This Basic Self-Care Checklist Will Help You Gauge How You Have Been Taking Care of Yourself."

6 Blogging, for example, emerges in the early 2000s among a sector of the Black community in college or working in jobs that provide the privacy of a cubicle or office, a personal computer, and enough time to regularly engage in long-form writing.

7 Author and scholar Candice Benbow (2016) compiled the *Lemonade Syllabus* as a reader to pair with Beyoncé's 2016 album. The syllabus contains two hundred suggestions for fiction and nonfiction readings.

8 Sean Carter (Jay-Z), the spouse of Beyoncé Knowles-Carter, released his studio album *4:44* in 2017, wherein he details struggles related to infidelity in their marriage and their reconciliation.

9 The Beyhive is the moniker for Beyoncé's fandom.

10 *Love & Hip Hop* is a reality show that airs on VH1 and documents the lives of hip-hop artists, producers, and managers. The show first aired in 2011.

11 Instagram has a "live" feature wherein users can stream video to followers and engage with them in real time.

12 President Bill Clinton was impeached in the House of Representatives in December of 1998, as Cardi B rightly asserts. However, he was not removed by the Senate and was found not guilty on both charges in the trial that followed.

13 The Jena Six were a group of Black teens convicted of assaulting a white classmate in Jena, Louisiana, in 2006 following incidents of racial violence and terrorism toward Black students at the school. The arrest and subsequent convictions sparked protests that were organized in part online. More than fifteen thousand protesters came from all over the country after organizing caravans to Louisiana using Facebook. The case demonstrated the power of social media organizing for young people long before Twitter activism became a topic for researchers.

## CONCLUSION

1 After the release of Cole's "Snow on tha Bluff," the hashtag #QueenTone trended on Twitter to mock and signify upon Cole's use of the word *queen* to describe the Black woman he went on to tone police in his lyrics.

2 Priscilla Slater was arrested by police after her boyfriend opened fire at a Detroit motel. Witnesses saw the man violently abuse Slater and drag her to the car where they were both found sleeping the next day. Rather than receiving medical attention, Slater was put in a holding cell where she later died in police custody.

3 See Fouché (2006).

4 Writing as Janie Crawford's nanny in her novel *Their Eyes Were Watching God*, Zora Neale Hurston writes, "De nigger woman is de mule uh de world so fur as Ah can see," pointing out the reliance of American society on Black women's labor (Hurston, 1990, p. 14).

# REFERENCES

Abidin, C. (2016). "Aren't these just young, rich women doing vain things online?" Influencer selfies as subversive frivolity. *Social Media + Society*, 2(2). https://doi.org/10.1177/2056305116641342.

Abrahams, R. (1999). The signifying monkey. In H. A. Ervin (Ed.), *African American literary criticism, 1773 to 2000*. Twayne.

Act to Prevent All Persons from Teaching Slaves to Read or Write, N.C.C. § 6 (1830). https://digital.ncdcr.gov.

Ajayi, L. (2016). *I'm judging you: The do-better manual*. Henry Holt.

Ajayi, L. [@luvvie]. (2018a, August 16). *Someone suggested Tevin Campbell to sing at Aretha's tribute. Under what rock did they pull that name from?* [Tweet]. Twitter.

Ajayi, L. [@luvvie]. (2018b, August 16). *Tevin Campbell is trending, Lawdt. I KNOW he can blow but I haven't heard his name in awhile. People took* [Tweet]. Twitter. https://twitter.com/Luvvie/status/1030501901194985472.

Ajayi, L. [@luvvie]. (2020, June 29). *I've been locked out of posting on my Awesomely Luvvie FB page for over a week. The last post on* [Tweet]. Twitter. https://twitter.com/Luvvie/status/1277664291341193218.

Ajayi, L. (2021). *Professional troublemaker: The fear-fighter manual*. Penguin.

Alexander-Floyd, N. G. (2012). Disappearing acts: Reclaiming intersectionality in the social sciences in a post-Black feminist era. *Feminist Formations*, 24(1), 1–25. https://doi.org/10.1353/ff.2012.0003.

Almánzaris, B. [@iamcardib]. (2017, September 28). *Bill Clinton got impeached for getting his dick sucked & this [carrot emoji] still president ruining the country in less* [Tweet]. Twitter. https://twitter.com/iamcardib/status/913374561680343041.

Aspegren, E. (n.d.). Transgender murders are "rampant" in 2020: Human Rights Campaign counts 21 so far, nearly matching total of a year ago. *USA Today*. Retrieved July 10, 2020, from www.usatoday.com.

Atwater, D. (2009). *African American women's rhetoric: The search for dignity, personhood, and honor*. Lexington Books.

Bailey, M. (2021). *Misogynoir transformed: Black women's digital resistance*. New York University Press.

Banks, A. J. (2010). *Digital griots: African American rhetoric in a multimedia age*. Southern Illinois University Press.

Banks, N. (2019, February 19). *Black women's labor market history reveals deep-seated race and gender discrimination*. Economic Policy Institute. www.epi.org.

Baraka, A. (1969). Technology and ethos. In *Raise, race, rays, raze: Essays since 1965* (1st ed.). Vintage.

Bell, B. W. (1987). *The Afro-American novel and its tradition*. University of Massachusetts Press.

Bellinger, W. (2007). Why African American women try to obtain "good hair." *Sociological Viewpoints, 23*, 63–72.

Benbow, C. (2016). *Lemonade syllabus*. Issuu. https://issuu.com.

Benjamin, R. (2019). *Race after technology: Abolitionist tools for the new Jim Code.* John Wiley & Sons.

Berger, J., & Milkman, K. L. (2012). What makes online content viral? *Journal of Marketing Research, 49*(2), 192–205. https://doi.org/10.1509/jmr.10.0353.

Berlin, I. (1974). *Slaves without masters: The free Negro in the antebellum South.* Pantheon.

Blake, J. (2020, July 17). *Why white supremacy is actually killing white people.* CNN. www.cnn.com.

Bonilla-Silva, E. (2006). *Racism without racists: Color-blind racism and the persistence of racial inequality in the United States.* Rowman & Littlefield.

Boyce-Davies, C. (2002). *Black women, writing and identity: Migrations of the subject.* Routledge.

Brezina, C. (2005). *Sojourner Truth's "Ain't I a woman?" speech: A primary source investigation* (1st ed.). Rosen Central Primary Source.

Bristol, D. W., Jr. (2009). *Knights of the razor: Black barbers in slavery and freedom.* Johns Hopkins University Press.

Brock, A. (2009). Life on the wire: Deconstructing race on the internet. *Information, Communication & Society, 12*(3), 344–63. https://doi.org/10.1080/1369118080266o628.

Brock, A. (2012). From the blackhand side: Twitter as a cultural conversation. *Journal of Broadcasting & Electronic Media, 56*(4), 529–49. https://doi.org/10.1080/08838151.2012.732147.

Brock, A. (2018). Critical technocultural discourse analysis. *New Media & Society, 20*(3), 1012–30. https://doi.org/10.1177/1461444816677532.

Brock, A., Jr. (2020). *Distributed Blackness: African American cybercultures* (Vol. 9). New York University Press.

Brown, C. M. "Lin." (1988). Comparison of typing and handwriting in "two-finger typists." *Proceedings of the Human Factors Society Annual Meeting, 32*(5), 381–85. https://doi.org/10.1177/154193128803200533.

Brown, K. M. (1998). Beyond the great debates: Gender and race in early America. *Reviews in American History, 26*(1), 96–123.

Brown, S. (2018). Delivery service: Gender and the political unconscious of digital humanities. In E. Losh & J. Wernimont (Eds.), *Bodies of information: Intersectional feminism and the digital humanities* (pp. 261–86). University of Minnesota Press. https://doi.org/10.5749/j.ctv9hj9r9.18.

Bruns, A. (2008). *Blogs, Wikipedia, second life, and beyond: From production to produs-age*. Peter Lang.

Bryant, T. (2018, July 25). Serena Williams hits out at frequency of her anti-doping tests. *Guardian*. www.theguardian.com.

Burgess, F. (1996). The white woman: The Black woman's nemesis. *Revue Française d'Études Américaines, 67*(1), 99–107. https://doi.org/10.3406/rfea.1996.1628.

Burnley, M. (2020, June 20). Author Brittney Cooper on harnessing rage, right now. *New York Times*. www.nytimes.com.

Burns, J. (2017, December 17). Black women are besieged on social media, and white apathy damns us all. *Forbes*. www.forbes.com.

Byers, D. (2016, February 27). *MSNBC's Melissa Harris-Perry walks off show in protest*. CNN Money. https://money.cnn.com.

Byrd, A., & Tharps, L. (2014). *Hair story: Untangling the roots of Black hair in America*. Macmillan.

Byrne, D. N. (2007). Public discourse, community concerns, and civic engagement: Exploring Black social networking traditions on BlackPlanet.com. *Journal of Computer-Mediated Communication, 13*(1), 319–40. https://doi.org/10.1111/j.1083-6101.2007.00398.x.

Carby, H. V. (1987). *Reconstructing womanhood: The emergence of the Afro-American woman novelist*. Oxford University Press.

Caswell, M. (2016). *Owning critical archival studies: A plea*. UCLA. https://escholarship.org.

Choney, S. (2018, March 13). *Why do girls lose interest in STEM? New research has some answers—and what we can do about it*. Microsoft News. https://news.microsoft.com.

Christopher, M. (2009). *On the court with . . . Venus and Serena Williams*. Little, Brown.

Clark, M. [@meredithclark]. (2020, July 18). *Earning wages for my intellectual labor is a fair and just practice; it is a normalized practice in this capitalistic* [Tweet]. Twitter.

Clarke, A. R. (2018, August 5). *The digital and Black hair: Technology and African material culture—sister from another planet*. Sister from Another Planet. www.sisterfromanotherplanet.com.

Coaston, J. (2019, May 20). *The intersectionality wars*. Vox. www.vox.com.

Cobb, J. (2016, March 14). The matter of Black lives. *New Yorker*. www.newyorker.com.

Cochrane, K. (2013, December 10). The fourth wave of feminism: Meet the rebel women. *Guardian*. www.theguardian.com.

Coleman, M. A., Cannon, K. G., Razak, A., Monroe, I., Majeed, D. M., Skye, L. M., Mitchem, S. Y., & West, T. C. (2006). Roundtable discussion: Must I be womanist? [With response]. *Journal of Feminist Studies in Religion, 22*(1), 85–134.

Collier, S. (2006). "And ain't I a woman?" Senegalese women immigrants, language use, acquisition, and cultural maintenance in an African hair-braiding shop. In J. Mugane, J. Hutchison, & D. Worman (Eds.), *Selected proceedings of the 35th annual conference on African linguistics, Somerville* (pp. 66–75). Cascadilla Proceedings Project.

Collins, P. H. (1989). The social construction of Black feminist thought. *Signs, 14*(4), 745–73. https://doi.org/10.1086/494543.

Collins, P. H. (2009). *Black feminist thought: Knowledge, consciousness, and the politics of empowerment* (2nd ed.). Routledge.

Collins, P. H., & Bilge, S. (2016). *Intersectionality*. Polity.

Colman, P. (1994). *Madam C. J. Walker: Building a business empire*. Millbrook.

Combahee River Collective. (1983). The Combahee River Collective statement. In B. Smith (Ed.), *Home girls: A Black feminist anthology* (1st ed., pp. 264–74). Kitchen Table: Women of Color Press.

Cooper, A. J. (1926, August 21). *Letter to George Jones*. MS. Mrs. George (Anna Julia Haywood) (Cooper Folder), Oberlin College Archives, Oberlin, OH.

Cooper, A. J. (2017). *A voice from the South: By a Black woman of the South*. University of North Carolina Press.

Cooper, A. J., Lemert, C. C., & Bhan, E. (1998). *The voice of Anna Julia Cooper: Including a voice from the South and other important essays, papers, and letters*. Rowman & Littlefield.

Cooper, B. C. (2016). Intersectionality. In L. Disch & M. Hawkesworth (Eds.), *The Oxford handbook of feminist theory* (pp. 385–406). Oxford University Press. https://doi.org/10.1093/oxfordhb/9780199328581.013.20.

Cooper, B. C. (2017). *Beyond respectability: The intellectual thought of race women*. University of Illinois Press.

Cooper, B. C. (2018). *Eloquent rage: A Black feminist discovers her superpower*. St. Martin's Press.

Crenshaw, K. (1990). Mapping the margins: Intersectionality, identity politics, and violence against women of color. *Stan. L. Rev., 43*, 1241–99.

CROWN Act. (n.d.). *About*. Retrieved July 4, 2020, from www.thecrownact.com.

Curry, A. [@ayeshacurry]. (2015, December 5). *Everyone's into barely wearing clothes these days huh? Not my style. I like to keep the good stuff covered up* [Tweet]. Twitter. https://twitter.com/ayeshacurry/status/673364404830777344.

Curtis, T. (2015). *New media in Black women's autobiography: Intrepid embodiment and narrative innovation*. Springer.

Dam, R., & Siang, T. (2019, January 1). *Stage 4 in the design thinking process: Prototype*. Interaction Design Foundation. www.interaction-design.org.

Daniels, J. (2009). Rethinking cyberfeminism(s): Race, gender, and embodiment. *Women's Studies Quarterly, 37*(1/2), 101–24. www.jstor.org/stable/27655141.

Davidson, M. del G. (2019). *Black women, agency, and the new Black feminism*. Routledge.

December, J. (1993, July 8). *Characteristics of oral culture in discourse on the net* [Paper presentation]. Penn State Conference on Rhetoric and Composition, University Park, PA, United States. www.december.com.

Dhamoon, R. K. (2010). Considerations on mainstreaming intersectionality. *Political Research Quarterly, 64*(1), 230–43. https://doi.org/10.1177/1065912910379227.

Dionne, E. (2017, April 10). If your beliefs are oppressive, you are not a feminist. *Harper's BAZAAR.* www.harpersbazaar.com.

Dixon, M. (2005). Hair braiding: Working the boundaries of methodology in globalisation research. *Qualitative Research Journal, 5*(1), 80–89.

D'Onofrio, K. (2015, July 20). *Women, minorities continually left behind in STEM jobs.* DiversityInc. www.diversityinc.com.

Dudley, G. (2013, January 10). In search of sisterhood: African American women's literary clubs in MARBL. *Rose Library Blog.* https://scholarblogs.emory.edu.

Durham, A. (2007). Using [living hip hop] feminism: Redefining an answer (to) rap. In G. Pough, E. Richardson, A. Durham, & R. Raimist (Eds.), *Home girls, make some noise! Hip hop feminism anthology* (pp. 304–12). Parker.

Durham, A., Cooper, B. C., & Morris, S. M. (2013). The stage hip-hop feminism built: A new directions essay. *Signs: Journal of Women in Culture and Society, 38*(3), 721–37. https://doi.org/10.1086/668843.

Everett, A. (2009). *Digital diaspora: A race for cyberspace.* SUNY.

Famuyiwa, R. (Director). (2002). *Brown sugar* [Film]. Fox Searchlight Pictures.

Faulconbridge, G. (2019, June 12). *The media has a big problem, Reuters Institute says: Who will pay for the news?* Reuters. www.reuters.com.

Flake, E. (2017, August 29). *As #BlackGirlMagic turns four years old, CaShawn Thompson has a fresh word for all the magical Black girls.* Blavity News & Politics. https://blavity.com.

Florini, S. (2013). Tweets, tweeps, and signifyin': Communication and cultural performance on "Black Twitter." *Television & New Media, 15*(3), 223–37. https://doi.org/10.1177/1527476413480247.

Florini, S. (2014). Recontextualizing the racial present: Intertextuality and the politics of online remembering. *Critical Studies in Media Communication, 31*(4), 314–26. https://doi.org/10.1080/15295036.2013.878028.

Florini, S. (2019). *Beyond hashtags: Racial politics and black digital networks.* New York University Press.

Ford, L. K. (2009). *Deliver us from evil: The slavery question in the old South.* Oxford University Press.

Foster, K. [@KimberlyNFoster]. (2019, May 7). *Ayesha is not the problem. She is the victim of the same shit the rest of us are dealing with* [Tweet]. Twitter.

Fouché, R. (2006). Say it loud, I'm Black and I'm proud: African Americans, American artifactual culture, and Black vernacular technological creativity. *American Quarterly, 58*(3), 639–61. https://doi.org/10.1353/aq.2006.0059.

Fowler, R. (1994). How the secondary orality of the electronic age can awaken us to the primary orality of antiquity or what hypertext can teach us about the Bible. *Interpersonal Computing and Technology: An Electronic Journal for the 21st Century, 2*(3), 12–46.

Franklin, C. W. (1985). The Black male urban barbershop as a sex-role socialization setting. *Sex Roles, 12*(9), 965–79. https://doi.org/10.1007/BF00288098.

Franklin, V. P. (1995). *Living our stories, telling our truths: Autobiography and the making of the African-American intellectual tradition.* Scribner.

Fraser, N. (1990). Rethinking the public sphere: A contribution to the critique of actually existing democracy. *Social Text, 25/26,* 56–80.

Freelon, D., McIlwain, C., & Clark, M. (2018). Quantifying the power and consequences of social media protest. *New Media & Society, 20*(3), 990–1011.

Freire, Paulo. (2006). The banking model of education. In Eugene F. Provenzo (Ed.), *Critical issues in education: An anthology of readings* (pp. 105–17). Sage. (Original work published 1970).

Gaskins, N. (2014, September 1). *Hair braiding is technology.* Recess. www.recessart.org.

Gates, H. L., Jr. (2014). *The signifying monkey: A theory of African American literary criticism* (25th anniversary ed.). Oxford University Press.

Giddings, P. (1984). *When and where I enter: The impact of Black women on race and sex in America* (1st ed.). W. Morrow.

Gill, T. M. (2010). *Beauty shop politics: African American women's activism in the beauty industry.* University of Illinois Press.

Grady, C. (2018, July 20). *The waves of feminism, and why people keep fighting over them, explained.* Vox. www.vox.com.

Gray, K. L. (2012). Deviant bodies, stigmatized identities, and racist acts: Examining the experiences of African-American gamers in Xbox Live. *New Review of Hypermedia and Multimedia, 18*(4), 261–76. https://doi.org/10.1080/13614568.2012.746740.

Gray, K. L. (2015). Race, gender, and virtual inequality: Exploring the liberatory potential of Black cyberfeminist theory. In R. A. Lind (Ed.), *Producing theory in a digital world: The intersection of audiences and production in contemporary theory* (pp. 175–92). Peter Lang.

Guy-Sheftall, B. (2009). Black feminist studies: The case of Anna Julia Cooper. *African American Review, 43*(1), 11–15.

Hancock, A.-M. (2016). *Intersectionality: An intellectual history.* Oxford University Press.

Hannah-Jones, N. (2019, August 18). The 1619 Project. *New York Times Magazine.* www.nytimes.com.

Hansen, M. B. N. (2006). *Bodies in code: Interfaces with digital media.* Routledge.

Haraway, D. J. (1985). Cyborg manifesto: Science, technology, and social-feminist in the late 20th century. *Social Review, 80,* 65–108.

Harris-Lacewell, M. V. (2010). *Barbershops, bibles, and BET: Everyday talk and Black political thought.* Princeton University Press.

Harris-Perry, M. (2008, February 8). Hillary's Scarlett O'Hara act. *Root.* www.theroot.com.

Higginbotham, E. B. (1993). *Righteous discontent: The women's movement in the Black Baptist Church, 1880–1920.* Harvard University Press.

hooks, b. (1992). Eating the other: Desire and resistance. In *Black looks: Race and representation* (pp. 21–39). South End.

hooks, b. (1994). *Teaching to transgress: Education as the practice of freedom*. Routledge.

hooks, b. (2000a). *Feminism is for everybody: Passionate politics*. Pluto Press.

hooks, b. (2000b). *Feminist theory: From margin to center*. Pluto Press.

hooks, b. (2016, May 9). *Moving beyond pain*. bell hooks Institute. https://web.archive.org/web/20201114005109/http://www.bellhooksinstitute.com/blog/2016/5/9/moving-beyond-pain.

Hughes, A. [Akilah Obviously]. (2015, April 8). *On intersectionality in feminism and pizza* [Video]. YouTube. www.youtube.com/watch?v=FgK3NFvGp58.

Human Rights Campaign. (2019). *Violence against the transgender community in 2019*. www.hrc.org.

Hunter, T. W. (2017). *Bound in wedlock: Slave and free Black marriage in the nineteenth century*. Belknap Press of Harvard University Press.

Hurston, Z. N. (1990). *Their eyes were watching God*. HarperCollins.

Hurston, Z. N. (2000a). Characteristics of Negro expression. In P. Swenson (Ed.), *African American literary theory: A reader* (pp. 31–44). New York University Press.

Hurston, Z. N. (2000b). How it feels to be colored me. In R. Giscon & E. Stoller (Eds.), *Worlds of difference: Inequality in the aging experience* (pp. 95–97). SAGE.

Hurston, Z. N. (2002). Hurston to Mason, October 15, 1931. In C. Kaplan (Ed.), *Zora Neale Hurston: A life in letters* (pp. 185–426). Doubleday.

Hurston, Z. N. (2006). *Their eyes were watching God*. Harper Perennial Modern Classics.

Hurston, Z. N., & Miles, R. (2018). *Barracoon: The story of the last "black cargo."* Amistad.

Jackson, D. A. (2018, August 8). Joan Morgan, hip-hop feminism, and the miseducation of Lauryn Hill. *Paris Review*. www.theparisreview.org.

Jackson, P. (2014, April 12). 7 reasons why men should watch Scandal according to an actual man. *Very Smart Brothas*. https://verysmartbrothas.theroot.com.

Jackson, P. (2017, August 18). How Trump ruined my relationship with my white mother. *Very Smart Brothas*. https://verysmartbrothas.theroot.com.

Jackson, S. J., Bailey, M., & Welles, B. F. (2020). *#HashtagActivism: Networks of race and gender justice*. MIT Press.

Jamilah Lemieux: Writer, speaker, fixer. (n.d.). *About*. Retrieved July 14, 2020, from www.jamilahlemieux.com.

Johnson, K. S. (2011). Political hair: Occupational licensing and the regulation of race and gender identity. *Du Bois Review: Social Science Research on Race, 8*(2), 417–40.

Jones, F. (2019a). *Reclaiming our space: How Black feminists are changing the world from the tweets to the streets*. Beacon.

Jones, F. [@FeministaJones]. (2019b, January 24). *Some of us feel we've been left to fend for ourselves against his relentless attacks . . . like ppl* [Tweet]. Twitter.

Jones, F. (2019c, February 8). *For CaShawn Thompson, Black girl magic was always the truth*. Beacon Broadside: A Project of Beacon Press.

Jones, F. [@FeministaJones]. (2019d, October 1). *In case you're wondering, they're talking about Jason Roger Pope, who was arrested for sex trafficking. They're DEMANDING that Blk* [Tweet]. Twitter.

Jones, F. [@FeministaJones]. (2019e, October 14). *I am realizing I get more engagement on Instagram and Facebook than I do via Twitter. I have 10x more* [Tweet]. Twitter.

Jun, P., & Ajayi, L. (2018, April 16). *Luvvie Ajayi on being generous with your work.* Own Your Content. https://ownyourcontent.wordpress.com.

Keister, L. A., & Southgate, D. E. (2012). *Inequality: A contemporary approach to race, class, and gender.* Cambridge University Press.

Kendall, M. (2020). *Hood feminism: From the women that a movement forgot.* Penguin Random House.

King, J. (2014, May 9). *Is Beyoncé a terrorist? Black feminist scholars debate bell hooks.* Colorlines. www.colorlines.com.

Lacy, K. R. (2004). Black spaces, Black places: Strategic assimilation and identity construction in middle-class suburbia. *Ethnic and Racial Studies, 27*(6), 908–30. https://doi.org/10.1080/0141987042000268521.

Lebsock, S. (1985). *The free women of Petersburg: Status and culture in a southern town, 1784–1860.* Norton.

Lee, C. D. (1993). *Signifying as a scaffold for literary interpretation: The pedagogical implications of an African American discourse genre.* National Council of Teachers of English. https://eric.ed.gov.

Lemieux, J. (2016, May 11). bell hooks and the sour "Lemonade" review. *Ebony Online.* www.ebony.com.

Lemieux, J. (2019a). R. Kelly's time is finally up. *Huffington Post.* www.huffpost.com.

Lemieux, J. [@JamilahLemieux]. (2019b, March 26). *I was the first person to edit some of your favorite writers* [Tweet]. Twitter.

Lemieux, J. [@JamilahLemieux]. (2019c, May 7). *Four years ago, she made a comment about modest clothing and folks have acted like she's the president of the* [Tweet]. Twitter. https://twitter.com/JamilahLemieux/status/1125786139703566336.

Lerner, G. (1973). *Black women in white America: A documentary history.* Vintage.

Levine, L. W. (2007). *Black culture and Black consciousness: Afro-American folk thought from slavery to freedom.* Oxford University Press.

Lindsey, T. (2014). Let me blow your mind: Hip hop feminist futures in theory and praxis. *Urban Education, 50*(1), 52–77. https://doi.org/10.1177/0042085914563184.

Lindsey, T. (2020, July 22). Why are Black women so often relegated to the margins? *Time.* https://time.com.

Loewen, J. W. (1988). *The Mississippi Chinese: Between Black and white.* Waveland.

Lorde, A. (1984). *Sister outsider: Essays and speeches.* Crossing.

Lorde, A. (2007). The master's tools will never dismantle the master's house. In *Sister outsider: Essays and speeches* (pp. 110–14). Crossing.

Lothian, A., & Phillips, A. (2013). Can digital humanities mean transformative critique? *Journal of E-Media Studies, 3*(1). https://doi.org/10.1349/PS1.1938-6060.A.425.

Lu, J. H. (2017). *Reckoning with freedom: Legacies of exclusion, dehumanization, and Black resistance in the rhetoric of the freedmen's bureau.* [Dissertation, University of Maryland]. https://drum.lib.umd.edu.

Lu, J. H., & Steele, C. K. (2019). "Joy is resistance": Cross-platform resilience and (re)invention of Black oral culture online. *Information, Communication & Society, 22*(6), 1–15. https://doi.org/10.1080/1369118X.2019.1575449.

Lucas, D. (2014a). *Don't waste your pretty*. Books by Belle.

Lucas, D. (2014b, December 17). 6 things I care about on "Beyoncé" more than her feminism. *A Belle in Brooklyn*. www.demetrialucas.com.

Luders-Manuel, S. (2015, August 12). What it means to be mixed race during the fight for Black lives. *For Harriet*. www.forharriet.com.

Mabee, C., & Newhouse, S. M. (1995). *Sojourner Truth: Slave, prophet, legend*. New York University Press.

Macklin, W. (1995, November 19). Supertypist Mavis Beacon is a creation of marketing. *Seattle Times*. www.seattletimes.com.

Marie Claire [@marieclaire]. (2014, April 2). *Kendall Jenner takes bold braids to a new epic level* [Tweet]. Twitter. https://twitter.com/marieclaire/status/451403750960562176?lang=en.

May, V. M. (2008). "By a Black woman of the south": Race, place, and gender in the work of Anna Julia Cooper. *Southern Quarterly, 45*(3), 127–52.

May, V. M. (2009). Writing the self into being: Anna Julia Cooper's textual politics. *African American Review, 43*(1), 17–34. www.jstor.org/stable/27802556.

McIlwain, C. D. (2019). *Black software: The internet and racial justice, from the AfroNet to Black Lives Matter*. Oxford University Press.

McNeill, L. (2017, February 7). These four Black women inventors reimagined the technology of the home. *Smithsonian*. www.smithsonianmag.com.

Mills, Q. T. (2014). *Cutting along the color line: Black barbers and barber shops in America*. University of Pennsylvania Press.

Mock, J. (2016, May 9). *Femme feminists/writers/thinkers/artists are consistently dismissed, pressured to transcend presentation in order to prove our woke-ability* [Status update]. Facebook. www.facebook.com/janetmock/posts/10154228113096522.

Moody-Turner, S. (2019). Prospects for the study of Anna Julia Cooper. *Resources for American Literary Study, 40*, 1–29. https://doi.org/10.5325/resoamerlitestud.40.2018.0001.

Morgan, J. (2000). *When chickenheads come home to roost: A hip-hop feminest breaks it down*. Simon & Schuster.

Morgan, J. (2018). *She begat this*. Simon & Schuster.

Morrison, T. (1971, August 22). What the Black woman thinks about women's lib. *New York Times*. www.nytimes.com.

Munro, E. (2013, September 5). *Feminism: A fourth wave?* The Political Studies Association (PSA). www.psa.ac.uk.

Nakamura, L. (2002). *Cybertypes: Race, ethnicity, and identity on the internet*. Routledge.

Nelson, A. (2020, January 31). *An interview with Alondra Nelson* (N. El-Hadi, Interviewer). *Believer*. https://believermag.com.

Newman, C. (2017, March 10). Chimamanda Ngozi Adichie on feminism. Interview by Cathy Newman. Channel 4 News UK [Television broadcast]. London, UK.

New School. (2014, October 7). *A public dialogue between bell hooks and Laverne Cox* [Video]. YouTube. www.youtube.com/watch?v=9oMmZIJijgY.

Noble, S. U. (2018). *Algorithms of oppression: How search engines reinforce racism.* New York University Press.

Noble, S. U., & Tynes, B. M. (2016). *The intersectional internet: Race, sex, class, and culture online.* Peter Lang.

Norton, M. B. (1984). The evolution of white women's experience in early America. *American Historical Review, 89*(3), 593–619. https://doi.org/10.2307/1856118.

Nouraie-Simone, F. (2005). Wings of freedom: Iranian women, identity, and cyberspace. In Fereshteh Nouraie-Simone (Ed.), *On shifting ground: Muslim women in the global era* (pp. 131–46). Feminist Press.

Nunley, V. (2011). *Keepin' it hushed: The barbershop and African American hush harbor rhetoric.* Wayne State University Press.

O'Brien, J. (Ed.). (1973). *Interviews with Black writers.* Liveright.

Ofori-Atta, A. (2011, March 21). Is hip-hop feminism alive in 2011? *Root.* www.theroot.com.

Omi, M., & Winant, H. (1998). *Racial formation in the United States* (3rd ed.). Routledge.

Omolade, B. (1987). A Black feminist pedagogy. *Women's Studies Quarterly, 15*(3/4), 32–39. www.jstor.org/stable/40022003.

*One of the best uses of Cardi B I've seen thus far.* (2017, October 17). [Facebook comment]. Facebook.

Ong, W. J. (1982). *Orality and literacy: The technologizing of the word.* Methuen.

Oppel, R. A., Gebeloff, R., Lai, K. K. R., Wright, W., & Smith, M. (2020, July 5). The fullest look yet at the racial inequity of coronavirus. *New York Times.* www.nytimes.com.

Owens, S. (2019, May 13). *A new study sheds light on what drives paid subscriptions for news.* Medium. https://medium.com.

Packnett, B. [@MsPackyetti]. (2017, January 29). *We have two hands: one is to battle, one is to build* [Tweet]. Twitter.

Papacharissi, Z. (2002). The virtual sphere: The internet as a public sphere. *New Media & Society, 4*(1), 9–27.

Papacharissi, Z. (2010). *A private sphere: Democracy in a digital age.* Polity.

Parham, M. (2018, December 17). *Signals, archives, digital Blackness* [Opening talk]. Digital Blackness in the Archive: A Documenting the Now Symposium, St. Louis, MA, United States.

Parham, M. (2019). *Sample | signal | strobe: Haunting, social media, and Black digitality.* Debates in the digital humanities. https://dhdebates.gc.cuny.edu.

Patton, T. O. (2006). Hey girl, am I more than my hair? African American women and their struggles with beauty, body image, and hair. *NWSA Journal, 18*(2), 24–51.

Pew Research Center. (2018, August 9). *An examination of the 2016 electorate, based on validated voters.* Pew Research Center—U.S. Politics & Policy. www.pewresearch.org.

Pomponi, S. (2020, June 12). We're sorry for not listening to Black influencers before: We expect to be called out. *Adweek.* www.adweek.com.

Prieger, J. E., & Hu, W.-M. (2008). The broadband digital divide and the nexus of race, competition, and quality. *Information Economics and Policy, 20*(2), 150–67. https://doi.org/10.1016/j.infoecopol.2008.01.001.

Randall, N. (1989, January). Mavis makes it easy. *Compute!, 11*(1), 70. www.commodore.ca.

Rettberg, J. W. (2014). *Blogging.* Polity.

Rheingold, Howard. (2000). *The virtual community: Homesteading on the electronic frontier* (Rev. ed.). MIT Press.

Roberts, M. (2013, May 3). Nobody has the right to deny you power over your body or your future. *TransGriot.* https://transgriot.blogspot.com.

Roberts, M. (2014, February 7). Moni ain't happy about the bigoted white trans feminine attack on Janet. *TransGriot.* https://web.archive.org.

Robertson, E. (2017, September 30). Intersectional-what? Feminism's problem with jargon is that any idiot can pick it up and have a go. *Guardian.* www.theguardian.com.

Robinson, C. L. (2011). Hair as race: Why "good hair" may be bad for Black females. *Howard Journal of Communications, 22*(4), 358–76.

Rockman. (2017). *An intimate look at Black Girls CODE: A case study of culturally-relevant coding programming and its long-term benefits.* Rockman. http://rockman.com.

Roediger, D. R. (2006). *Working toward whiteness: How America's immigrants became white: The strange journey from Ellis Island to the suburbs.* Hachette.

Rosenblatt, K. (2018, August 22). *Louisiana girl sent home from school over braided hair extensions.* NBC News. www.nbcnews.com.

Ross, T. (2016, March 3). An open letter to Melissa Harris-Perry from a grateful student. *Root.* www.theroot.com.

Savage, R. (2019, August 9). Want to have a hot-girl summer? Start by supporting sex workers. *Bitch Media.* www.bitchmedia.org.

Shackelford, A. (2016). #BlackTransLivesMatter: How Black cis-women are part of the problem. *For Harriet.* http://ashleighshackelford.com.

Shammas, C. (1985). Black women's work and the evolution of plantation society in Virginia. *Labor History, 26*(1), 5–28. https://doi.org/10.1080/00236568508584783.

Shilton, K. (2003). *"This scholarly and colored alumna": Anna Julia Cooper's troubled relationship with Oberlin College.* Oberlin College.

Shine. (2020, February 7). *The Black women of Shine HQ on self-care, self-love, and more.* https://advice.theshineapp.com.

Smith, A. (2010). *Mobile access 2010.* Pew Internet and American Life Project. www.pewinternet.org.

Smith, C. A. (2005). *Market women: Black women entrepreneurs—past, present, and future.* Greenwood.

Sollee, K. (2015, October 30). 6 things to know about 4th wave feminism. *Bustle*. www .bustle.com.

Spillers, H. J. (1987). Mama's baby, papa's maybe: An American grammar book. *Diacritics*, *17*(2), 65–81.

Squires, C. R. (2002). Rethinking the Black public sphere: An alternative vocabulary for multiple public spheres. *Communication Theory*, *12*(4), 446–68. https://doi.org/ 10.1111/j.1468-2885.2002.tb00278.x.

Steele, C. K. (2018). Black bloggers and their varied publics: The everyday politics of Black discourse online. *Television & New Media*, *19*(2), 112–27.

Stenberg, A. [@amandlastenberg]. (2015, July 12). *When you appropriate Black features and culture but fail to use your position of power to help Black Americans by* [Comment] Instagram. www.instagram.com/p/5AWcLYHGty.

Sterling, D. (1997). *We are your sisters: Black women in the nineteenth century*. W. W. Norton.

Stringfield, R. (2020, January 10). *"Brown sugar" was more than a love story. It's an ode to Black feminism*. Zora. https://zora.medium.com.

Sutherland, T. (2017). Archival amnesty: In search of Black American transitional and restorative justice. *Journal of Critical Library and Information Studies*, *2*, 1–23.

Tasker, Y., & Negra, D. (2007). *Interrogating postfeminism: Gender and the politics of popular culture*. Duke University Press.

Tate, C. (1983). *Black women writers at work*. Continuum.

Tate, S. (2007). Black beauty: Shade, hair and anti-racist aesthetics. *Ethnic and Racial Studies*, *30*(2), 300–319.

Taylor, Y. (2019). *Zora and Langston: A story of friendship and betrayal* (1st ed.). W. W. Norton.

Telusma, B. (2020, September 25). *Activist Tamika Mallory slams Daniel Cameron: "You are a coward, you are a sellout."* Grio. https://thegrio.com.

*This picture really bothers me. Someone should have said center Breonna Taylor. She seems like an afterthought. Design really matters.* (2020, July 7). [Tweet]. Twitter.

Thomas, L. (1998). Womanist theology, epistemology, and a new anthropological paradigm. *Cross Currents*, *48*(4). www.crosscurrents.org.

Thompson, C. (2009). Black women, beauty, and hair as a matter of *being*. *Women's Studies*, *38*(8), 831–56. https://doi.org/10.1080/00497870903238463.

Thornton, C. (2019, December 26). Black girls with braids banned from Harlem production of Black Nutcracker. *Black Enterprise*. www.blackenterprise.com.

Tiidenberg, K. (2018). *Selfies: Why we love (and hate) them*. Emerald.

Tomlinson, B. (2018). The vise of geometry: Distorting intersectionality at the scene of argument. *Meridians*, *16*(1), 1–36. https://doi.org/10.2979/meridians.16.1.03.

Turkle, S. (1997). Seeing through computers. *American Prospect*, *8*(31), 76–82.

Walker, A. (1983). *In search of our mothers' gardens: Womanist prose* (1st ed.). Harcourt Brace Jovanovich.

Walker, A. (2004). *In search of our mothers' gardens: Womanist prose*. Houghton Mifflin Harcourt.

Wallace, M. (1999). *Black macho and the myth of the superwoman.* Verso.

Walton, A. (1999, January). Technology versus African-Americans. *Atlantic, 283*(1), 14–18.

Walton, N., & Carter, E. T. (2013). *Better than good hair: The curly girl guide to healthy, gorgeous natural hair!* HarperCollins.

Waters, M. C. (1990). *Ethnic options: Choosing identities in America.* University of California Press.

Weld, T. D. (Ed.). (1839). *American slavery as it is: Testimony of a thousand witnesses.* American Anti-Slavery Society.

Wells-Barnett, I. B. (1895). *A red record: Tabulated statistics and alleged causes of lynchings in the United States, 1892–1893–1894.* Donohue & Henneberry.

Wells-Barnett, I. B., DeCosta-Willis, M., & Washington, M. H. (1995). *The Memphis diary of Ida B. Wells.* Beacon.

Wells-Barnett, I. B., Ewing, E. L., & Duster, M. (2020). *Crusade for justice: The autobiography of Ida B. Wells* (A. Duster, Ed., 2nd ed.). University of Chicago Press.

White, D. G. (1999). *Ar'n't I a woman? Female slaves in the plantation South.* W. W. Norton.

Whitlock, J. (2009, July 9). *Serena could be the best ever, but . . .* Fox Sports. http://web.archive.org.

Williams, F. B. (1987). The colored girl. In M. H. Washington (Ed.), *Invented lives: Narratives of Black women, 1860–1960* (1st ed., pp. 150–59). Anchor.

Williams, J. (2017, May 12). Wearing braids gets Black girls banned from prom at Massachusetts school. *Newsweek.* www.newsweek.com.

Williams, S. (2015). Digital defense: Black feminists resist violence with hashtag activism. *Feminist Media Studies, 15*(2), 341–44.

Wolcott, V. W. (2001). *Remaking respectability: African American women in interwar Detroit.* University of North Carolina Press.

Wood, P. H. (1996). *Black majority: Negroes in colonial South Carolina from 1670 through the Stono Rebellion.* Norton.

Young, D. (2016, September 29). How being ashy in public is actually underrated, explained. *Very Smart Brothas.* https://verysmartbrothas.theroot.com.

Young, D. (2017a, July 17). Why we joined Gizmodo Media Group (GMG), explained. *Very Smart Brothas.* https://verysmartbrothas.theroot.com.

Young, D. (2017b, September 19). Straight Black men are the white people of Black people. *Very Smart Brothas.* https://verysmartbrothas.theroot.com.

Young, D. (2018a, August 8). The 10 ashiest people in America, ranked. *Very Smart Brothas.* https://verysmartbrothas.theroot.com.

Young, D. (2018b, September 21). A look back at the reaction to "Straight Black men are the white people of Black people" a year later. *Very Smart Brothas.* https://verysmartbrothas.theroot.com.

Zimman, L., Davis, J., & Raclaw, J. (2014). *Queer excursions: Retheorizing binaries in language, gender, and sexuality.* Oxford University Press.

Ziv, S. (2020, July 2). June jobs report shows uneven recovery; Black unemployment still tops 15 percent. *Forbes.* www.forbes.com.

# INDEX

Bold page numbers refer to images

Bitch Media, 146

Black blogosphere, 1, 17–18, 42, 67, 73, 88, 147, 157. *See also* blogging

Black cyberfeminism, 8, 15

*Black Enterprise*, 73

Black feminism as product, 18, 22, 55, 63, 104, 121–48, 156

Black feminist pedagogy, 139

Black feminist praxis, 3, 8–9, 13, 55, 93, 140, 146–47, 155–56; genealogies of, 12, 18, 95–122, 153; hip-hop feminism and, 10, 59, 161n5

Black feminist shades of gray, 10, 52, 57–59, 63, 68–70, 157

Black Girl Magic, 6–7

Black Girls CODE, 1–2, 31

Black internet studies, 50, 164n6

Black Lives Matter. *See* Movement for Black Lives / Black Lives Matter

Black nationalism, 52

*Black Nutcracker*, 46

BlackPlanet, 73, 125, 166n7

Black technophilia, 17, 52, 61–63

Black technophobia, 60–62, 147

Black Twitter, 50, 62, 66–67, 104, 106–7, 164n6, 165n3

Black vernacular technological creativity, 62, 96

Bland, Sandra, 91

Blogger, 65, 165n2

blogging, 2, 22, 49, 63–64, 87–89, 96, 109, 125–26, 133, 139, 151, 162n7; agency and, 68–72; comments sections, 67, 73–76, 81–85, 90; hair blogs, 3, 17, 41–42, 65, 147; influencers and, 164n4; lifestyle blogs, 3, 17, 48–49, 81, 100; methodology and, 12, 155–57; microblogging, 118; nonbinary gender in, 76–80; patriarchy and, 80–85; relationship blogs, 17; relationship to social media, 2, 65–67, 137; self-identification in, 73–76, 131. *See also* Black blogosphere; virtual beauty shop; vlogging; *individual bloggers and blogs*

Blogspot, 73, 165n2

Bonilla-Silva, Eduardo, 166n9

Boone, Sarah, 162n3

boring work, 120–21

braiding, 41, 44–47, 140

branding, 48–49, 66, 100, 104, 111, 168n5, 169n3; of Black feminism, 18, 130, 132; as employment requirement, 79; personal, 73–74, 85, 105, 113, 125, 130–33, 143–46

Bravo, 68, 126

Brock, André, 7, 66, 165n11; on Black cyberculture, 50–51, 62, 164n6; on Black Twitter, 106–7; on critical technocultural discourse analysis, 161n6; on ratchetry, 168n7

Brown, Kathleen, 162n1

Brown, Michael, 86, 90

*Brown Sugar*, 123–24

Bruns, Axel, 66

Bryant, Kimberly, 1. *See also* Black Girls CODE

Burgess, François, 27

Burke, Tarana, 87, 119

Burns, Janet, 4

Burr, Liz, *Very Smart Brothas (VSB)*, 80–85

Burroughs, Nannie Helen, 36

BuzzFeed, 137, 169n5

call-and-response, 84–85

Cameron, Daniel, 91

Campbell, Tevin, 104

capturing, 99, 153; as Black feminist praxis, 18, 101–9, 121

Carby, Hazel, 27

Cardi B (Belcalis Marlenis Almánzaris), 143–46, 170n12

Carter, Sean. *See* Jay-Z (Sean Carter)

Chappelle, Dave, *Chapelle's Show*, 126–27

Chauvin, Derek, 149

Cherry, Matthew, *Hair Love*, 65, 67

Children's Defense Fund, 116

civil rights movement, 9, 87, 98, 117, 162n1
Civil War (US), 37, 45, 162n3, 164n12
Clark, Meredith, 66, 138
Clarke, Andréa Rose, 46
Clinton, Bill, **145**
Clinton, Hillary Rodham, 89, 161n3, 170n12
*Clutch*, 112
coding, 1–3, 31, 65–66
Cole, J., 150
Coleman, Monica, 14
Collins, Patricia Hill, 10–11, 21, 23, 30, 74, 84, 157; on matrix of domination, 17, 52–56, 101; on womanism, 14
colonialism/imperialism, 10, 34, 64, 132, 138; anti-, 57; British, 51; European, 26; pre-, 23; Spanish, 164n3; US, 16, 61
colorism, 50, 63
Combahee River Collective, 4, 53, 132
controlling images, 30, 54, 72, 131
Cook, Maya and Deanna, 46
Cooper, Anna Julia, 18, 36, 100, 109, 115, 155, 168n8; *A Voice from the South*, 110–12
Cooper, Brittney, 3, 9, 53, 57, 84, 150, **154**; *Eloquent Rage*, 131; on hip-hop feminism, 57–58; on race women, 37, 56
counterpublics, 7, 42, 49, 82, 85, 87, 164n2, 168n10
COVID-19, 149
Cox, Laverne, 78–79, 166n13
Creative Commons, 78
Crenshaw, Kimberlé, 10, 52–54, 84
Crews, Terry, 119
critical archival studies, 24
critical technocultural discourse analysis (CTDA), 161n6
CROWN Act, 41
#CROWNDay, 41
Crunk Feminist Collective (CFC), 58
Cullors, Patrisse, 86. *See also* Movement for Black Lives / Black Lives Matter
cult of true womanhood/domesticity, 27–29, 34, 150–51, 163n6

cultural appropriation, 44–45, 140–42
Cunningham, Brittany Packnett, 33, **154**
Curry, Ayesha, 135–37
Curry, Stephen, 135
Curtis, Tracy, 8
cyberfeminism, 14; Black, 8, 15
cyber studies, 14
cyborgs, 14, 62

Dam, Rikke, 144
Daniels, Jessie, 14–15
Davidson, Maria del Guadalupe, 71, 139, 153
Davies, Carole Boyce, 10
Deen, Paula, 107
#DefundThePolice, 87
Delany, Samuel, 61
Denmark, 11
DeRogatis, Jim, 169n12
Dery, Mark, 61
digital Black feminism, definition, 13
digital divide, 7, 50, 60, 164n6
digital praxis, 3, 112, 156
digital studies, 4, 15, 152
digital turn, 3, 12, 38, 59
Disqus, 76
DJs, 62
domestic violence, 69, 150, 166n6
dragging, 104
Durham, Aisha, 9, 57

eating the other, 140–42
*Ebony*, 111–12
editing, 82, 100, 109, 111–12
Elgin, Ellen, 162n3
emancipation, 35, 37, 42, 61, 67, 97, 125, 153, 162n1, 164n12
England, 26, 29
entrepreneurship, 44–45, 47–50, 70, 71
*Essence*, 112
Esu Elegbara, 127
ethics, 12–13, 155–57, 168n8
Eurocentrism, 41, 84

## ABOUT THE AUTHOR

Catherine Knight Steele is Assistant Professor of Communication at the University of Maryland, College Park, with affiliate appointments in the American Studies Department, the Maryland Institute for Technology in the Humanities, and the Harriet Tubman Department of Women, Gender, and Sexuality Studies.